THE MAN TRAPS

RECLAIM YOUR POWER AND INTUITION IN RELATIONSHIPS

KALASHREE SENGUPTA

Clever Fox® PUBLISHING

Chennai • Bangalore

CLEVER FOX PUBLISHING
Chennai, India

Published by CLEVER FOX PUBLISHING 2026

ISBN: 978-93-7500-539-1

Dedicated To:

The women learning to trust their inner voice and unwavering truth.

And the men courageous enough to meet life from vulnerability and the wisdom of their heart.

"No tree can grow to heaven unless its roots reach down to hell."

– Carl Jung

CONTENTS

PROLOGUE

You Are Not Broken

Most women are not broken.

They are exhausted.

Exhausted from loving men who cannot meet them.

Exhausted from confusing emotional chaos with spiritual destiny.

Exhausted from stories that promise salvation through another person.

For centuries, women have been told that somewhere in the world, there exists a man who will complete them.

A soulmate.

A cosmic counterpart.

A twin flame.

A love so powerful it feels written in the stars.

A love that explains every longing, every heartbreak, every moment of loneliness.

It is a beautiful story.

It is also one of the most dangerous myths women have inherited.

Because the twin flame myth does something subtle and devastating.

It persuades you that your wholeness exists outside of you.

It convinces you to tolerate confusion in the name of destiny.

It romanticises emotional chaos as spiritual growth.

And it keeps you chasing intensity while quietly abandoning yourself.

For years, I believed this myth.

I searched for love across continents, across relationships, across heartbreaks that nearly dismantled me.

Each time believing that the next man might finally be the one.

The one who would make everything make sense.

But the truth revealed itself slowly, painfully, and through experiences that forced me to confront patterns I had been unconsciously repeating.

The Man Traps was born from that awakening.

It is a map of the relational archetypes I encountered, the illusions they revealed, and the deeper psychological and spiritual patterns beneath them. This book is not an attack on men.

It is an invitation into awareness.

Because once you see the patterns clearly, they lose their power.

And once you stop abandoning yourself for love, the traps stop working.

You are not waiting for someone to complete you.

You are waiting to remember your own sovereignty.

And that is where this journey begins.

PREFACE

The Twin Flame Myth: Breaking the Illusion

I grew up addicted to a fantasy.

Even as a little girl, long before I understood the mechanics of love or the depth of longing, I believed there was a man out there who was mine.

My cosmic counterpart.

My destined half.

My twin flame.

On long car rides with my father, mountains flashing past like ancient witnesses, I would press my forehead to the window and imagine that great love — the one that would somehow make the world feel safe, meaningful, and complete.

But life had forged a very different path for me.

I was not meant for a soft landing.

I was meant for collision.

My life did not hand me a prince or a pedestal. It handed me fire — mental fire, emotional fire, spiritual fire, physical fire, sexual fire, even financial fire.

I was not raised to be rescued.

I was forged through experience.

Every heartbreak became a mirror.

Every betrayal became a teacher.

Every relationship became a doorway back to myself.

This is not a victim's story.

This is a story of awakening.

For over a decade, I have worked with women navigating trauma, intuition, and the complex emotional terrain of modern relationships. Through healing sessions, retreats, and deep personal work, I began noticing a striking pattern.

The same dynamic appeared again and again.

Brilliant women.

Sensitive women.

Deeply intuitive women.

All caught in relationships that felt magnetic, spiritual, and impossible to walk away from — even when those relationships were quietly draining their power. They would say things like:

"I know something feels wrong… but I can't explain it."

"He says we're twin flames."

"I feel like I've known him in another lifetime. This is karmic."

And almost always, beneath the language of destiny, there was something else at work.

Confusion.

Manipulation.

Trauma bonds dressed up as spiritual connection.

This pattern became impossible for me to ignore.

The Man Traps was born not only from the women I worked with, but from the patterns I lived through myself.

Because before I became the woman guiding others through these traps, I walked through them myself.

Repeatedly.

Painfully.

And often blindly.

I take full ownership of the men I drew toward me- the karmic magnets, the spiritual con artists, the broken boys dressed as awakened men. They were not accidents. They were initiations. They cracked me open so I could walk out of the ruins with one brutal revelation blazing in my chest:

No one completes you.

No one saves you.

You are the one you've been waiting for. We have all heard these words. But I offer lived experience of the word "SELF-RELIANCE," which to me is beyond self-love. It's when you adorn the crown and the sword. You become all that you were waiting for. You land in yourself.

This journey was not linear; it was intense and even sometimes a maze of sorts. My higher self would scream from within, “Come home to yourself”, while my human self would chase after yet another failure of a date or another illusory relationship disaster. This dichotomy and split led to a lot of friction in my being. The higher self is complete; it is the human self that needs and yearns for love as if it’s the salvation. The irony is that the salvation is within, not without.

My process was merging my human self with my higher self.

Twice, I fell into the abyss- two seismic collapses, what mystics call the dark night of the soul. Each collapse was triggered by love, or by the absence of it. My marriage to a gentle-seeming American environmentalist became a silent warzone of addiction, violence, and emotional decay. I left it with nothing but a backpack, a passport, and a heart so shattered it could barely hold its own rhythm. I wandered through Sri Lanka like Meera searching for Krishna, walking bare feet, looking at each man with that glimmer of hope, convinced my twin flame was still out there- the missing half of my soul.

But here is the truth I bled for:

The twin flame myth is not a destiny-

It is a trap wrapped in spiritual poetry.

An illusion that seduces you into believing your wholeness is outside you.

It convinces you to tolerate red flags in the name of “divine union.”

It keeps you chasing a fantasy while abandoning yourself.

This book is a rebellion against that lie.

It is a psycho-spiritual roadmap drawn from my ashes- the archetypes of men I encountered, the shadows they activated, the traps they represented, and the lessons my soul demanded I learn. These men were not villains; they were the catalysts. They showed me the invisible patterns that secretly govern attraction, trauma, and the dance between the masculine and feminine energies. When I say men and women, I refer to all those who identify as primarily masculine or primarily feminine.

Each chapter reveals an archetype- the charm, the chaos, the unravelling, and the alchemy. My intention is not to judge but to illuminate. It is to hand you the lantern I never had, so you don't wander into the same darkness blind. Because awareness doesn't just change your relationships- it rewires your destiny.

If you are reading this, you are not here by accident.

You are here because something in you is ready to wake up.

This book is for the women who love too hard, too intensely.

Who forgive too often.

Who mistake intensity for intimacy.

Who lose themselves in the dreams of men who barely know themselves.

It is for the empaths who become prey.

For the seekers who become lost.

For the lovers who forget they are sovereign.

The patterns are not gendered- the pain belongs to everyone.

This book is not just for women who have lost themselves in love.

It is also for men who are ready- truly ready- to look inward.

For the men who feel the weight of their own unspoken wounds.

For the men who understand that strength is in realising their vulnerability.

For the men who want to rise- not in dominance, but in integrity.

For the men who know that avoiding their shadows is what keeps them small, reactive, defensive and disconnected.

For the men who desire a new paradigm of relating- one built not on games, masks, or emotional evasion, but on emotional presence, accountability, and inner alignment.

Because true intimacy is not built through performance or projection.

It is built through inner work.

This book calls both masculine and feminine energies back into consciousness- into awareness, honesty, and sovereignty - so that relationships may evolve from toxic patterns into elevated, embodied connection.

If you are reading this, you are not here accidentally.

Your soul is asking for a deeper truth. Welcome to The Man Traps. May these pages crack you open, shake you awake, and deliver you- fiercely- back to yourself.

This book is the light that illuminates all those traps. So, you may have the guidance that I never did.

INTRODUCTION

Who Am I?

I am Kalashree.

A woman forged in fire, sculpted by shadow, and tempered in the alchemy of my own becoming.

Today I work as a trauma-informed healer and writer, helping women understand the psychological and energetic patterns that shape their relationships. My work focuses on the intersection of trauma, intuition, embodiment, and the unseen dynamics that govern human connection. Most importantly, my work is about bringing women back to their inner knowing, their own truth and deep wisdom.

But these roles were not handed to me.

I bled my way into them.

My childhood was wrapped in privilege and punctuated by emotional absence.

I grew up between airports and forests, luxury hotels and lonely bedrooms. My father taught me how to read the silence of nature — to track birds, to trace the shape of a falling leaf, to understand the wild as a mirror.

My mother, a brilliant lawyer, taught me what ambition sounds like when spoken by a woman in a world that resists her voice.

And yet, in the gaps between their brilliance and their busyness, something essential was missing.

I was raised largely by nannies, not nurturers.

Sick days were often the only moments that bought my mother's attention.

That is how abandonment plants itself — quietly, systematically, almost politely — until it becomes part of the architecture of a child's inner world.

I remember constantly asking my father as a child,

"Are you angry with me?"

Because when tension existed between my parents, I felt responsible for it. And thus, the triangulation was born, somehow, I became the peacekeeper.

I internalised their conflict until much later in life, when something inside me finally erupted with a force I could no longer suppress.

The rage of Kali.

The moment I stopped being the peacekeeper and began becoming the pattern breaker.

My earliest memories of childhood were not the gentle safety we associate with innocence.

Some of my first experiences of the world carried confusion and pain far too large for a child to understand.

At the age of three, I went through an experience that deeply affected my sense of safety and innocence. Home was not always a refuge either. As a child, I often absorbed emotional realities far beyond my years — adult grief, adult conflict, and emotional burdens no child should have to carry.

My mother, struggling with her own unresolved pain, sometimes leaned on me emotionally in ways that were difficult for a child to understand or hold.

At times her anger spilled outward.

At other times it dissolved into denial.

For years I was caught in the confusing space between truth and silence — learning early that reality can be distorted when people refuse to face their own wounds.

On a soul level, however, I understand something now that I did not understand then.

My mother showed me what happens when a woman abandons herself.

My father showed me what betrayal does to love.

Together they taught me what I would never become.

I carry both the mother wound and the father wound.

Some days I wonder which cuts deeper.

But the truth is this:

Both were necessary.

Both accelerated my becoming.

I did not choose parents who would cradle me.

I chose parents who would crack me open so fiercely that I would be forced to find my own divinity.

From them, I learned sovereignty.

From them, I learned that waiting for external love is one of the most dangerous myths a woman can believe.

So, who am I?

I am the woman who took every fracture and forged it into a framework of power.

I am the child who survived her parents' storms and grew her own sunlight.

I am the healer who walks into the dark without flinching because I was raised in its basement.

I am the writer who names the wounds others bury.

And I am here to remind women of something their bones already know:

You do not need to be rescued. You need to remember who you are.

THE KALI MANIFESTO- The Feminine Rises

This is not simply Kalyug.

This is Kali Yug.

The age when illusion burns.

The age when truth refuses to remain buried.

The age when the feminine remembers her power.

For centuries women were taught to soften themselves before speaking truth.

To be agreeable before sovereign.

To endure before being free.

We inherited a silent contract:

Love deeply.

Forgive endlessly.

Endure quietly.

And we were told that this was virtue.

But something is changing.

Across the world women are waking away from the spell.

They are recognising the difference between love and conditioning.

Between intimacy and control.

Between spiritual language and spiritual manipulation.

Because once a woman sees clearly, she cannot return to blindness.

The body has always known.

It knows when energy feels unsafe.

It knows when affection carries control.

It knows when intuition is warning, not imagination.

For generations women were taught to override that knowing.

To rationalise danger.

To silence instinct.

To make excuses for what their nervous system recognised as harm.

Those days are ending.

The feminine is no longer here to be prey.

She is here to be sovereign.

The feminine is not weak.

She is life itself.

The Creator. Nurturer. Protector.

And when necessary — the destroyer of illusion.

Kali does not apologise for her power.

She cuts through deception.

She exposes the truth.

She burns away what is false so something real can rise.

To awaken the Kali within is not to become cruel.

It is to become clear.

Clear about what you will tolerate.

Clear about who has access to your energy.

Clear about the difference between love and manipulation.

And when that clarity arrives, everything changes.

Women stop romanticising emotional chaos.

They stop confusing intensity with intimacy.

They stop believing pain is proof of love.

They stop abandoning themselves to maintain connections.

And perhaps most importantly—They stop waiting to be chosen.

The awakened feminine chooses herself.

She chooses truth over illusion.

Self-respect over temporary affection.

Clarity over confusion.

This is not a war against men.

It is a return to balance.

Because when women stop abandoning themselves, the world must evolve.

The old paradigm cannot survive in the presence of the conscious feminine power.

Only integrity can.

Only presence can.

Only truth can.

This is Kali Yug.

The age when the feminine remembers.

And once she remembers, nothing can make her forget again.

Rise, woman.

Kali walks with you, and through you.

The world remembers her power.

A Reader's Roadmap

How to Move Through This Book

This book is not meant to be consumed quickly.

It is meant to be entered consciously.

What you are holding is not a dating manual, a self-help checklist, or a spiritual manifesto. It is a psycho-spiritual road map of relating—designed to help you recognise patterns before they cost you your body, your voice, or your sense of self.

Many of us were taught how to attract love.

Very few of us were taught how to recognise danger disguised as desire, or how to listen to the body when it whispers before it screams.

This book exists so you do not walk into relationships blind.

The Core Philosophy of This Book

At the heart of this work is a simple but radical truth:

Healing in relationships cannot occur without awareness—

and awareness cannot occur without accountability.

This book does not position men as villains and women as victims.

It examines relational dynamics, psychological patterns, and somatic responses—with compassion, clarity, and responsibility.

You will be invited to look at:

- The psyche of certain relational traps- such as the narcissistic trap that we know all so well, or even better and more rampant, the flakster trap
- The shadow patterns of the men who embody them
- And equally importantly, your own internal patterns (as I have examined my own) that made these dynamics familiar, tolerable, or attractive

Not to shame yourself.

But to free yourself.

At the end of each chapter, the work turns inward. Having named and examined the pattern, we move from intellectual recognition to somatic awareness—because the body often knows the trap long before the mind is willing to admit it. Through simple, somatic and trauma-informed exercises, readers are guided to perceive how each dynamic registers in the nervous system: the subtle tightening in the chest, the collapse in the belly, the buzzing urgency to please, or the familiar freeze that accompanies self-betrayal. These practices are not about fixing or overriding the body, but about restoring trust in its signals.

As readers learn to identify what misalignment feels like in real time, discernment becomes embodied rather than reactive. The work gently retrains the nervous system to associate safety with consistency, presence, and reciprocity—rather than intensity, unpredictability, or emotional labour. Over time, the compulsion to chase, explain, or over-give begins to dissolve, replaced by a grounded sense of self-containment.

The book does not promise a partner as a reward for healing. Instead, it offers something more enduring: wholeness. From this integrated state—where boundaries are felt, needs are honoured, and intuition is trusted—attraction naturally shifts to alignment. Relationships are no longer chosen from survival or scarcity, but from clarity and resonance. What emerges is not the pursuit of an idealised other, but the capacity to meet partnership from a place of stability, self-respect, and emotional sovereignty.

Aligned connection, in this framework, is not something to manifest—it is something the nervous system recognises.

How Each Chapter Is Structured (And Why)

Each chapter follows the same psycho-spiritual architecture, so your nervous system learns how to recognise patterns—not just understand them intellectually.

Think of every chapter as a map of a specific terrain.

1. The Anecdote: Entering the Trap

Each chapter begins with a lived anecdote—my direct experience inside a particular relationship.

This is intentional.

Stories bypass intellectual defences and speak directly to the body. As you read, you may feel resonance, discomfort, recognition, or resistance. All of that information matters.

You are not being asked to compare lives.

You are being asked to notice sensation.

2. The Psyche of the Man Trap

From the anecdote, we move into the psychological architecture of the particular man trap.

This section answers questions like:
- How does this type of dynamic typically form?
- What drives the behaviour beneath the surface?
- Why does it initially feel compelling rather than dangerous?

This is not about diagnosing men.

It is about recognising relational blueprints.

3. Shadow Patterns of the Man Trap

Here, we name the recurring behaviours that define the trap.

These shadow patterns are not always dramatic.

Often, they are subtle, gradual, and socially normalised.

You will begin to see how:
- Charm replaces consistency
- Intensity replaces intimacy
- Control replaces care

This section is meant to sharpen perception, not create fear.

4. My Own Patterns: Radical Self-Accountability

This is one of the most important sections of every chapter.

Healing cannot occur if responsibility is outsourced.

In this part, I turn the lens inward and ask:

- What wounds in me resonated with this dynamic?
- What unmet needs made this pattern familiar?
- What did I ignore, override, or rationalise?

This is not self-blame.

This is self-honesty.

You are not responsible for abuse.

You are responsible for learning what allowed you to stay.

This distinction is essential for liberation.

5. The Somatic Checklist: Detection Through the Body

Because danger is rarely logical, each chapter includes a somatic pattern recognition checklist.

These checklists help you learn to:

- Read bodily responses
- Identify early warning signs
- Distinguish activation from attraction
- Sense safety versus familiarity

The body is treated as an intelligent ally—not a problem to override.

You are encouraged to pause, breathe, and reflect as you move through these sections.

6. Concluding Truths & Takeaways

Each chapter ends with distilled truths—not prescriptions.

These are not rules for dating.

They are principles for discernment.

They are meant to:

- Settle the nervous system
- Anchor clarity
- Leave you with something you can carry forward

You may want to reread these sections slowly.

How to Read This Book (Very Important)

You do not need to read this book in one sitting.

In fact, it is better if you don't.

Some chapters may activate memory, grief, anger, or bodily sensations. This does not mean something is wrong. It means recognition is occurring.

You are invited to:

- Take breaks
- Journal
- Pause when emotions arise
- Read one chapter at a time

This book respects the reader's nervous system.

The Final Arc: From Pattern Recognition to Sovereignty

The book does not end by leaving you hyper-vigilant or closed off.

The final chapters and concluding section widen the lens to answer a deeper question:

What does wholeness actually look like—

And how do you recognise the real thing when it arrives?

Rather than offering fantasy or idealised relationships, we explore:

- What sovereignty feels like in the body
- How wholeness changes attraction
- How safety feels different from intensity
- How love shows up without urgency, pressure, or confusion

This is not about perfection.

It is about grounded discernment.

Sovereignty is not independence from love.

It is independence from self-abandonment.

The Intention of This Book

This book will not tell you who to love.

It will teach you how to:

- See clearly
- Listen deeply
- Trust your body
- Honour your boundaries
- And stop repeating patterns that cost you your peace

The goal is not cynicism.

The goal is clarity.

So that when something real arrives,

you do not mistake it for boredom,

and you do not walk past it chasing intensity.

A Gentle Invitation

Read this book slowly.

Let it meet you where you are.

Awareness is not a destination.

It is a practice.

And this book is meant to walk with you

as you learn to practice seeing—

clearly, kindly, and without abandoning yourself.

The Man Traps Framework

A Map of the Archetypes You Will Encounter in This Book

Before entering the stories in this book, it helps to see the landscape clearly.

The men described in these pages are not random individuals. They represent recurring relational archetypes — patterns of behaviour that appear across cultures, cities, and generations.

Different faces.

Different professions.

Different personalities.

Yet beneath the surface, the same relational dynamics repeat.

These are what I call The Man Traps.

A Man Trap is not simply a difficult man. It is a psychological and relational pattern in which a man's unresolved wounds, avoidance, entitlement, manipulation, or predatory behaviour gradually erodes a woman's clarity, intuition, and sovereignty.

Many of these traps do not appear dangerous at first.

In fact, they often feel magnetic, intriguing, spiritual, intelligent, or emotionally compelling.

But beneath the surface lies a repeating pattern.

This book explores ten of the most common ones.

Recognising them is the first step toward breaking the cycle.

The Ten Man Traps

1. The Abusive Man-Child Trap

A man emotionally frozen in adolescence. Unable to regulate anger or take responsibility, he lashes out through rage, addiction, blame, or volatility. His partner gradually becomes both caretaker and target.

2. The Flaky Flaksters Man Trap

Charming, exciting, and initially attentive — but fundamentally incapable of consistency or commitment. He thrives on novelty and attention while avoiding responsibility or emotional depth.

3. The Cyber-Scam Man Trap

A manipulator who operates through digital identity, distance, or deception. Emotional intimacy, spirituality, or opportunity become tools to gain trust, attention, money, or access.

4. The Sexual Abuse Man Trap

A man who violates boundaries through coercion, pressure, manipulation, or entitlement. He treats a woman's body as something owed rather than honouring consent.

5. The Narcissistic Man Trap

The master of charm and psychological manipulation. He idealises you at first, then slowly devalues you while distorting reality to maintain control and superiority.

6. The Trauma Bond Man Trap

A man who creates powerful emotional dependency through cycles of affection and withdrawal. Moments of connection are followed by pain, creating addictive attachment that feels like love.

7. The Pseudo-Spiritual Man Trap

A man who weaponises spirituality. He speaks of awakening, tantra, consciousness, or divine connection while bypassing accountability and using spiritual language to gain control or access.

8. The Zero-Accountability Man Trap

A man incapable of self-reflection. Conflict is always someone else's fault. Growth, responsibility, and repair never occur.

9. The Advice-Giving Man Trap

A man who positions himself as a guide, mentor, therapist, or authority. Instead of relating as an equal partner, he maintains control by constantly analysing, correcting, or instructing.

10. The Psychopathic Pathological Liar Man Trap

A man who constructs entire realities through deception. Identities, stories, promises, and emotions become tools of manipulation.

These archetypes are not meant to label individuals permanently.

They are meant to illuminate patterns.

Because once a pattern becomes visible, it loses much of its power.

Before continuing into the chapters, take a moment to reflect honestly on your own experiences.

The following diagnostic exercise will help you recognise which pattern may have appeared in your life.

The Man Traps Diagnostic Test

Which Archetype Are You Dealing With?

Relationships rarely reveal their patterns immediately. What often appears as attraction, chemistry, or even spiritual connection can slowly reveal deeper psychological dynamics.

This exercise is designed to help you recognise patterns early.

For each question, choose the answer that feels closest to your experience.

Write down the letter you select each time.

At the end, count which letter appears most often to discover which Man Trap archetype may be present.

Question 1

How did the relationship begin?

A. He was charming but inconsistent from the start. Plans changed frequently.

B. He showered you with admiration and attention very quickly.

C. The connection felt intense, almost addictive.

D. He immediately pushed sexual boundaries or escalated intimacy too fast.

Question 2

How does he behave when you ask for clarity?

A. He says things like "Let's just go with the flow."

B. He becomes defensive or dismissive.

C. He alternates between warmth and distance.

D. He shifts the conversation into spiritual or philosophical language.

Question 3

How does conflict usually unfold?

A. He disappears or becomes vague.

B. He blames you or refuses responsibility.

C. He apologises but repeats the behaviour later.

D. He tries to analyse you and give advice rather than listen.

Question 4

How does he position himself in the relationship?

A. As someone who wants freedom and no labels.

B. As someone superior or always right.

C. As someone wounded who needs your empathy.

D. As a mentor, guide, or authority figure.

Question 5

How does your body feel most of the time around him?

A. Anxious and uncertain about where you stand.

B. Small, criticised, or psychologically destabilised.

C. Addicted to the highs and lows of the connection.

D. Confused because spiritual language is mixed with discomfort.

Question 6

How does he treat truth and honesty?

A. He avoids direct answers.

B. He gaslights you by rewriting events or distorting reality.

C. He promises change but his behaviour never shifts.

D. You later discover major lies or fabricated stories.

Question 7

How does intimacy evolve?

A. He enjoys closeness but avoids commitment.

B. He uses affection to gain control.

C. Intense closeness is followed by withdrawal.

D. He pushes sexual intimacy regardless of your readiness.

Question 8

How does he respond to your personal growth?

A. He becomes distant when things deepen.

B. He feels threatened by your independence.

C. He pulls you back into emotional chaos.

D. He uses spirituality to justify behaviour.

Question 9

What role do you find yourself playing?

A. The patient one waiting for clarity.

B. The one defending your reality.

C. The rescuer or caretaker trying to heal him.

D. The student listening to his advice.

Question 10

What eventually becomes clear over time?

A. He never truly commits.

B. The relationship revolves around his ego.

C. The bond feels addictive but painful.

D. His stories, identity, or behaviour contain serious deception.

Scoring Your Results

Count which letter you chose most often.

Mostly A

The Flaky Flaksters Man Trap

A pattern of inconsistency, avoidance of commitment, and emotional ambiguity.

Mostly B

The Narcissistic Man Trap

A dynamic built on control, manipulation, and distorted reality.

Mostly C

The Trauma Bond Man Trap

A cycle of emotional highs and lows that creates addictive attachment.

Mostly D

Look at which description fits best:

- If spirituality is frequently used → Pseudo-Spiritual Man Trap
- If sexual boundaries were pressured → Sexual Abuse Man Trap
- If he constantly positions himself as the expert → Advice-Giving Man Trap
- If deception and fabricated stories dominate → Psychopathic Pathological Liar Man Trap

A Final Note

This exercise is not meant to diagnose anyone.

Its purpose is awareness.

Patterns become visible when we slow down and observe them honestly.

And the moment you can name a pattern clearly, you are already one step closer to stepping out of it.

CHAPTER 1

THE ABUSIVE MAN-CHILD TRAP

I married young. I was only twenty-three.

Let's call him D.

At that time, I believed I was finally claiming the freedom my soul longed for. My parents had been against the relationship from the start, which only made me want it more. I was determined to prove that I could choose love on my own terms.

But what I didn't realise then was that I wasn't choosing love. I was repeating pain.

The Good Girl Who Followed the Script

My early years were, in many ways, idyllic. I worshipped my parents beyond God. Before every exam, I would touch their feet. I was academically brilliant, disciplined, and obedient. We went on family trips, and I learned Indian classical music and dance. My father provided for us, and my mother took care of me when I was sick.

She wasn't the homey, nurturing kind, but she gave me something else- my command over language, my fierce intellect. My father, a businessman, expected me to study finance and economics at Boston University, then head to Harvard for an MBA and come back to make crores in our family consulting firm.

But my soul had other plans.

At seventeen, I got attuned to Reiki. My energy centres opened, and something deep within me awakened- a creative, intuitive current that refused to stay buried. I wanted to study creative writing, psychology, philosophy- anything that explored the invisible dimensions of life.

That was the beginning of the rift.

The more I tried to walk my soul's path, the more disconnected I became from my family's expectations.

The First Fire: My Mother's Rage

I was the perfect child- the over-achiever, the topper, the captain, the one who never faltered. Excellence was my shield; performance, my spell for protection. But even gold-plated childhoods rust under pressure.

When my parents' marriage cracked open- when my father's indiscretions became the ghost in every room- my mother collapsed inward. Depression hollowed her out, rage spilt outward, and I, at nine years old, became both therapist and punching bag. And when her pain overflowed, her hands found my flesh- bruising it, rewriting my body as a map of inherited hurt.

And then came the worst part- she forgot it all.

Or pretended to.

Denial is its own brutality. Her delusions got the better of her. And the worst part of it was that I was called mad, gaslit beyond belief. For speaking the truth, I was called insane.

Her anger was volcanic. Her hands were strong. My petite body bore the marks of her pain.

By sixteen, something inside me snapped. I told her that if she ever hit me again, I would hit back. That day, she stopped- but by then, two things had already happened:

1. I had developed an intense tolerance to abuse.
2. I had been robbed of my childhood.

And so, I learned early that love could hurt, and that truth could be erased.

Today, she is a shadow of the woman she was- unkempt, immobile, drowning in her own unresolved sorrow. And I stand in the complex space between compassion and distance. I have resorted to acceptance. Twenty-five years is too long to wait for someone to rise. I refuse to sink into the quicksand she mistook for comfort.

The Living Room War

Like a knight in shining armour, or so I thought, D and his mother came to Bombay to meet my family before the wedding. The scene is etched in my memory- sharp, hot, unblinking.

A living room. Two couches facing each other like battling rams.

D, his mother, and I on one side.

My parents- my birth family- on the other.

My father's face had gone a violent shade of red, the kind that comes before storms. His nose twirling, like it did before he was about to spew poison.

His voice cracked in the air.

"I can have you and your family put away. Don't forget the pull I have in this city."

D shot up straight, already in fight mode.

"You treat her like this, and you wonder why she wants to leave?"

My mother didn't even look at him. Her eyes were locked on me- cold, dissecting, familiar.

"This ungrateful girl. She'll leave you, too.

Just like she's leaving us."

Her words landed like a curse.

A seed she planted in his mind that would sprout in the darkest places of our marriage, for years.

I remember staring at her, unable to move, unable to speak.

Shock can be paralysing.

Or a disassociation.

Maybe both. I remember almost floating above this scene, unable to digest the gravity and reality of what was unfolding.

Then- the ripping sound.

Rrrrriip.

My mother had grabbed the envelope containing my fiancé visa documents.

The one marked in bold red: DO NOT OPEN UNTIL BEFORE AN IMMIGRATION OFFICER.

She tore it open with theatrical fury, like she was unravelling my future with her bare hands.

I lunged forward, too late.

"Maa! What are you doing? I waited ten months for this document." This was the first time I had felt rage, so grave, at the sheer violation of her act.

But she was already photocopying the papers, as if cataloguing evidence for a crime I had committed.

The crime being: choosing my own life.

Later, at the US Consulate, we would be told this was "not unusual."

Parents in India, in "fits of drama," tear open immigration documents- it happened more often than anyone wanted to admit.

But in that living room, everything felt singular.

Catastrophic.

Personal.

My parents moved in perfect toxic choreography- tearing down my character, guilt-tripping, and emotional blackmail.

They had a way of collapsing my sense of self until I felt like a shadow of a daughter.

A disappointment.

A sin with a heartbeat.

Some days, the heaviness made me wonder if removing myself entirely- from their lives, even from existence itself- would be a relief.

But a small, stubborn ember inside me stayed lit.

I never crossed that line.

Instead, something else happened that afternoon.

As the shouting bounced off the walls, I felt myself lift.

Literally.

I floated out of my body, into a strange, suspended vantage point above the room.

An astral balcony seat.

Watching the four of us reenact a karmic tragedy, a travesty in the making.

From up there, everything was suddenly clear.

This wasn't love. This was possession.

This wasn't protection. This was control disguised as concern.

This wasn't family. This was a cage.

The only door out was marked: Leave. Now.

And so, in that suspended, surreal moment-

Right or wrong, I chose what I thought was love.

Not sacred union, not aligned partnership.

Just the idea of love.

My version of it then:

the forbidden fruit.

I decided to elope and I shot up straight, ready to get out the door.

From the Frying Pan into the Fire

When I met D in college, I mistook attraction for safety. He was charming, adventurous, and a little wild. He exhibited anger issues even then, but I brushed them aside- convinced that love could heal anything.

After three years of dating, we married in the US and the energy shifted immediately. It's strange how marriage can reveal what was always hiding beneath the surface. On the very night of our wedding, I felt a wave of emptiness. The attraction vanished. My body knew before my mind did that something was terribly wrong.

Then the verbal abuse began. "You fucking cunt," he would say- almost daily. Soon came the hitting. And yes, sometimes, I hit back. But mostly, I froze. I was terrified, ashamed, and too proud to admit I had made a huge mistake.

I told no one.

The Descent

He drank heavily. He watched porn obsessively. He wanted to enact his fantasies on me, and when I refused, he mocked me. The more I grew spiritually- studying tantra, healing, energy work- the more he regressed into darkness.

I would speak of sacred union; he would joke about "putting his balls on my third eye." This was the starkness of the contrast between us.

The crudeness still echoes in my mind- more so because of what the act symbolised: the desecration of the sacred feminine, the humiliation of divinity through the body- the sheer disregard and disrespect.

There's a particular cruelty in being spiritually awake in an abusive relationship. You see the soul of the other person, you sense their pain, and you keep believing you can heal them. You think if you just love harder, forgive more, it will change.

It never does.

The Psychological Bridge-From Childhood to Marital Abuse

It took me many years to understand that childhood does not simply disappear behind us.

It becomes the architecture of our attraction.

The relationships we enter as adults often mirror the emotional terrain we first learned to survive as children.

Not consciously.

But somatically.

The body remembers what the mind tries to forget.

If love in childhood meant walking on eggshells, tension can later feel strangely intimate.

If care arrived braided with anger, volatility can masquerade as passion.

If truth was denied, distorted, or rewritten, you may grow up doubting your own perception of reality.

None of this happens because we seek pain.

It happens because the nervous system is trying—again and again—to resolve an unfinished story.

So, when I met D, I believed I was choosing a man.

In truth, I was stepping into a landscape my body already recognised.

Not love.

Familiarity.

And familiarity, when it is shaped by trauma, can feel indistinguishable from destiny.

The Cycle of Abuse

There's a pattern to it-one I now recognise clearly:

1. Tension builds- the silence, the looks, the walking on eggshells.
2. Explosion- the abuse erupts in words, fists, or threats.
3. Apology and remorse- tears, empty promises, declarations of change.
4. Spurts of the honeymoon phase- tenderness returns, temporarily.
5. The quiet before the next storm.

And every time you forgive, your tolerance for pain increases and the abuse worsens. Because silently, you just agreed to a higher tolerance of abuse. The cycle then further tightens its grip.

I repeated and stayed in this dizzying, soul-fracturing cycle for four years.

Why? Because trauma bonds feel like love. Because I was still that little girl who confused danger with home. And because even amidst all the violence, we would cuddle through the night, and that physical comfort became my drug.

Shadow Patterns of the Abusive Man-Child

In hindsight, D wasn't a man. He was a wounded boy trapped in a man's body- angry at the world, addicted to distraction, unable to grow.

Here are the signs I now see clearly in this archetype:

1. An intense, unresolved bond with the mother- often enmeshed or overdependent.
2. Unexpressed anger- projected onto the partner.
3. Addictions- alcohol, porn, drugs, or work as a form of escape.
4. Deep dissatisfaction- with his own life, choices, or sense of masculinity.
5. No accountability- always someone else's fault.
6. Lack of true self-reflection- no real desire to evolve.
7. A recurring abuse cycle- apology, charm, then repeat.

The Awakening

My awakening came not in a single moment, but through a spiritual rescue. The day came, and my higher self, decided that I had enough, and it just got me the hell out of that marriage through a spontaneous kundalini awakening. I knew then that I could either keep dying slowly in that house or walk away with nothing and begin again.

So, I left- with a backpack, some bruises, and a soul that had begun to see clearly.

My Takeaway

Abuse doesn't begin with the first slap or insult. It begins the moment you silence your intuition. My co-dependency and silence perpetuated the abuse.

When you ignore the tightening in your chest, the dissonance in your body, the moments when something doesn't feel right- that's when the erosion begins.

And if you grew up normalising pain, you will unconsciously seek it until you choose differently.

My lesson from D was brutal but sacred:

Love that hurts is not love. I was so used to abuse that I felt at home in it.

Love that diminishes you is not divine.

Love that silences you is toxic

Guidance for the Reader

If you recognise yourself in any of this- pause.

Watch for the early signs:

- How does he handle anger?
- Does he self-reflect or deflect and become defensive?
- Does he respect your spiritual and emotional growth, or mock it?
- Does he take accountability, or make you his emotional mother?

You cannot rescue a man who refuses to see his own wounds. You can only rescue yourself.

How the Abusive Man-Child Hooks Women

The abusive man-child does not arrive as a villain. He arrives as familiar.

He arrives with intensity, chemistry, urgency, and longing.

This archetype hooks women through trauma bonding by speaking a language that she at once identifies as familiar. What then ensues is a powerful neurological and emotional loop where moments of connection are interspersed with withdrawal, anger, or abuse. It starts small- snapping in the morning over a cup of coffee; then before you know it, you are getting socked in the face.

The nervous system becomes addicted to the highs and lows. Relief feels like love. Apologies feel like intimacy. Chaos masquerades as passion.

For women who grew up normalising emotional neglect, volatility, or even abuse, this dynamic feels strangely like home. The body recognises the rhythm even when the soul vehemently protests. And the ultimate tragedy here is that most women who find themselves in this situation come from abusive homes; they have nowhere else to go, so they succumb further in this quicksand of a dynamic.

The man-child often presents as wounded, misunderstood, or "different with you." He mirrors your empathy and vulnerability early on, creating the illusion of a deep connection. Slowly, subtly, the dynamic shifts. You begin managing his moods. You soften your truth to avoid explosions. You become smaller to keep the peace.

What is often missed is this truth:

Trauma does not seek peace. It seeks familiarity.

If abuse or emotional unpredictability was present in your formative years, your system may unconsciously gravitate towards relationships that recreate the same emotional landscape. Not because you want pain, but because your nervous system is trying to resolve an old wound using a familiar script.

This is how the hook sets:

- You feel chosen
- You feel special
- You feel needed
- And slowly, you feel trapped

Why the Pattern Repeats: What It Is Asking You to Heal

When a pattern repeats, it is not punishment- it is instruction.

If you find yourself repeatedly drawn to abusive or emotionally unavailable men, the question is not "What is wrong with them?" but rather:

What part of me is still organised around pain?

Unhealed trauma seeks reenactment.

Co-dependency seeks purpose.

An unsafe nervous system seeks regulation- anywhere it can find it.

Many women leave abusive homes or relationships only to unconsciously enter another version of the same dynamic. The faces change. The story doesn't.

Ask yourself honestly:

- Have I fully processed the abuse, or have I simply escaped it? If the answer is that you have escaped it then another abusive dynamic is almost guaranteed.
- Am I choosing this relationship from wholeness- or from survival?
- Is this partnership love, or is it my rescue plan?

This is a crucial distinction.

If you are looking for a man to:

- Save you
- Stabilise you
- Make you feel safe
- Prove your worth

Then the wound is still active.

The greatest red flag is not his behaviour- it is your hope that he will heal you.

When safety has not been cultivated internally, we seek it externally. We tolerate what harms us because chaos feels better than abandonment. We confuse endurance with devotion.

The pattern repeats until the lesson is embodied. In different forms, I repeated this exact pattern with different archetypes for thirteen years until something in me unlocked. My co-dependency, safety wounds and my need for validation. Once I came home to myself through intense hypnotherapy work and the realisation that I was indeed enough, I took complete accountability for healing my inner-child and never again did I leave her at the hands of a callous man again.

The Growth Path: Somatic Awareness & Nervous System Truth

Healing from the abusive man-child pattern is not cognitive alone. Insight is not enough. The body must be included.

Abuse lives in the nervous system.

If your body learned that love equals tension, vigilance, or walking on eggshells, then peace may initially feel boring- or even threatening. This is why somatic awareness is essential. Your body and nervous system are your radars for safety.

Start here:

- How safe do I feel in my body around this person?
- Do I relax- or brace- when he enters the room?
- Does my breath deepen, or shallow?
- Can I express discomfort without fear of retaliation, defensiveness or even rage?

The body does not lie.

True growth begins when you prioritise felt safety over fantasy.

When you listen to the tightening in your chest before your mind explains it away.

When you trust your discomfort more than his charm.

Healing is not about becoming stronger.

It is about becoming safer within yourself.

When safety becomes your baseline, abusive dynamics lose their grip. They no longer feel magnetic. They feel repellent.

The Hidden Pitfall: Rising Tolerance & Escalating Abuse

One of the most dangerous aspects of this pattern is tolerance.

Each time abuse is rationalised, minimised, or forgiven without change, the nervous system recalibrates. What once felt unacceptable becomes normal. What once shocked you now barely registers.

And abuse does not stay static- it escalates. It intensifies. That curse word now becomes a blow to the head.

The man-child's unresolved rage, entitlement, and emotional immaturity intensify over time. What begins as emotional volatility can evolve into psychological, financial, sexual, or physical harm.

The tragedy is this:

The more abuse you survive, the more capable you become of surviving even worse.

This is not strength- it is conditioning.

Breaking the cycle requires a radical recalibration of standards:

- Pain is not proof of love
- Endurance is not intimacy or strength
- Chaos is not passion
- Silence is not "keeping the peace"

The moment you feel yourself adjusting to harm is the moment to pause.

Ask:

- What am I tolerating now that I would never want my daughter or younger self to endure?
- Am I becoming less alive in this relationship?
- Am I shrinking to survive?

Freedom begins when you choose yourself before the breaking point.

The Abusive Man-Child Somatic Recognition Checklist

(A Nervous-System–Based Self Inquiry)

1. How does your body respond around him- especially when things are "good"?
   - Do you feel relaxed, open, and grounded?
   - Or alert, hyper-aware, waiting for the mood to change?

   If your body rarely feels at ease, your system is already signalling danger, even if your mind is romanticising it.
2. When he is upset, what role do you instinctively step into?
   - Do you feel compelled to soothe, explain, manage, or fix his emotions?

- Do you fear his anger or withdrawal?

  If you become his regulator instead of an equal partner, the man-child dynamic has already begun.

3. How does he respond when you express discomfort or a boundary?
   - Does he pause, reflect, and take responsibility?
   - Or does he deflect, minimise, mock, blame, or become defensive?

   Defensiveness in place of accountability is a core marker of emotional immaturity.
4. Are you mistaking intensity or chemistry for love?
   - Do the highs feel euphoric and the lows destabilising?
   - Does reconciliation feel more bonding than consistency?

   This is trauma bonding- not intimacy. Love does not require recovery periods.
5. Do you find yourself explaining away behaviour you would warn another woman about?
   - "He didn't mean it."
   - "He had a hard childhood."
   - "He's just stressed."

   The moment you become his interpreter to yourself; you are already carrying more than your share.
6. Does he respect your growth, spirituality, or emotional awareness?
   - Or does he subtly belittle, mock, compete with, or dismiss it?

   A man threatened by your evolution will unconsciously try to shrink you to stay comfortable.

7. Are you hoping this relationship will finally make you feel safe, chosen, or whole?
   - Does being with him feel like an escape from loneliness, chaos, or past pain?

   If this partnership feels like a rescue plan rather than a conscious choice, the wound is still active.
8. How does conflict actually resolve between you?
   - Is there sustained change and learning?
   - Or apologies, charm, promises—and repetition?
   - A repeating cycle without transformation is not repairable. It is a rehearsal.
9. Have you had to silence parts of yourself to keep the relationship stable?
   - Your needs, instincts, anger, voice, or truth?

   Love that requires self-abandonment is not love- it is survival.
10. If nothing changed, truly, could you live this way for five more years?
    - In your body?
    - In your spirit?
    - In your sense of self?

Your answer is your truth. Do not negotiate with it.

How to Read Your Responses

- If 3 or more questions activated discomfort: Pause. Something requires attention.
- If 5 or more resonated deeply: You are likely in- or entering- the Abusive Man-Child trap.

- If most answers came from tension, justification, or hope rather than safety: This dynamic is already shaping you.

Closing Truth

You cannot rescue a man who refuses to face his own wounds.

But you can rescue the parts of you that learned to confuse pain with belonging. And that was exactly what I did. I rescued myself from the burning building that was my marriage. I didn't know it yet, but that was my first step in choosing myself over the paradigm of systemic abuse that had been my battleground for the first three decades of my life.

This trap exists not to shame you- but to awaken you.

When you heal, the pattern ends.

When you choose safety, the cycle dissolves.

When you stop abandoning yourself, abusive love loses its power.

And that is not just healing- that is liberation.

CHAPTER 2

THE FLAKY FLAKSTERS MAN TRAP

We live in a world where situationships have replaced good old-fashioned romance, and sex has replaced sincerity. I have personally walked through a whole maze of "almost relationships"- dressed up as love, disguised as commitment, packaged as destiny, but hollow on the inside. They were flaky, non-committal, and emotionally unavailable. Yet they knew exactly how to mirror back my deepest needs: stability, devotion, partnership.

They sensed it like predators smell fear. They reflected my longing for love… then vanished the moment their physical or emotional needs were met.

And here's what baffled me:

There are plenty of women who want casual connections, so why do men still concoct elaborate lies? Why distort truth, manipulate emotions, and break hearts when there is a whole buffet of willing participants?

Why do they keep adding negative karma to their own journey?

One after another, I was met with illusory love that shattered within days or weeks. And every time, I gathered the wreckage of my heart and walked back into the arena- my human self stubbornly wanting to hold on to the belief that love could be found outside of me.

You see, self-love was a mythical unicorn for me. A poetic concept I didn't quite believe in. So, life kept testing me. Hard.

Heartbreak after heartbreak.

Until I finally learned to provide for myself in every way- emotionally, mentally, spiritually, physically.

The Psychology of a Flaky Man- The Shadow-Side

A flaky personality has very clear signs:

- They don't show up consistently.
- Their vocabulary is full of words like:

"Let's see."
"Let's explore."
"We'll figure it out."

- Zero commitment.
- Zero accountability.
- They take you lightly, stand you up, or treat plans like optional suggestions.

And the truth? Men are getting away with this because women allow it, or should I say, they settle into this trap. "If I am not getting a relationship, let me just settle into a situationship, they say to themselves." Not intentionally - but because we're conditioned to be patient, understanding, flexible, and hopeful.

The Flaksters Trap

Unfortunately, the modern dating landscape is intensely populated with what I call Flaksters- men who want novelty without responsibility, intimacy without presence, and access without accountability.

They are not confused.

They are not "finding themselves."

They are not overwhelmed by emotion, like they make you believe that they are. "Oh my god, I'm triggered," is the fastest-moving line they use. They are simply tourists in other people's hearts.

The Flakster philosophy is deceptively simple:

"Let's not complicate things."

Which roughly translates to: "I want access to your body, your time, your attention- but none of your expectations, needs, or reality."

Women, on the other hand, often enter dating with a very different orientation. Stability. Safety. Emotional availability. Growth. A shared direction. Not necessarily marriage on date one- but at least the dignity of being taken seriously as a human being, not a pit stop.

And here lies the mismatch:

Women are looking to build.

Flaksters are looking to consume.

The Road Trip Delusion

Flaksters love metaphors like "going with the flow."

They say it with the confidence of someone floating down a lazy river, forgetting that relationships are not inflatable tubes- you don't just drift and see where you end up.

To them, dating is a road trip.

No destination.

No map.

No responsibility for the passengers.

They will:

- Make pit stops
- Change playlists
- Pick up hitchhikers
- Drop you off when the conversation gets real

And when you ask, "Where is this going?" they look genuinely offended, as if you've asked them to file taxes on a Sunday afternoon.

Scene One: G — The Disappearing Gentleman

G arrived exactly as my nervous system prefers men to arrive: tall, salt-and-pepper beard, long hair that suggested both wisdom and artistic emotional unavailability. The kind of man who looks like he might quote Rumi and then forget to text back for three days.

We met at a café. Neutral ground. Safe lighting. Low expectations.

The date itself was… fine. Pleasant enough. Conversation flowed. Nothing alarming- except the subtle but unmistakable absence of effort. When the bill arrived, he stared at it like it was a philosophical question.

We split it.

Because feminism.

Or equal rights.

Or some vague idea that chivalry is now oppressive.

Now, let me be clear: women are not gold diggers for noticing effort. We are pattern readers. And effort tells a story.

Afterwards, as the evening wrapped up, I waited- standing slightly to the side- for him to at least pause. Ask how I was planning to go home. Offer to wait until my Uber arrives. Perhaps even- dare I say- offer a ride.

He did none of those things.

He got into his car and whizzed off. Just gone. A clean exit. Like a magician disappearing behind smoke, except the smoke was my disbelief.

And yet- because Flaksters always circle back- he called days later.

"Hey, baby," he said. Now I am his baby, apparently. The gall!

As if nothing had happened.

As if absence were a minor weather condition.

Then came the flakiness. The vanishing when conversations turned real. The sudden busyness. The gentle implication that I was intense- code for "you are asking for basic continuity."

And just like that, the script completed itself:

Approach. Withdraw. Reappear. Repeat. I swear they have learnt these patterns somewhere. And I would really like to know who trains these buffoons.

Scene Two: T — The Spiritually Enlightened Flakster

Then there was T.

T practised Isha meditation. He had a voice-over artist's voice- deep, confident, professionally intimate. The kind of voice that makes you swoon, and you then make the grave mistake of thinking he might be grounded, reflective, and evolved.

Spoiler alert: He was none of the above.

On our very first conversation- before we had even met- he casually announced that if we were in person, we would already be sleeping together.

Not flirted.

Not hinted.

Declared!

I remember staring at my phone, wondering where men acquire this level of nerve. Is it a course? A podcast? A secret Telegram group titled "How to Say the Most Unhinged Things with Confidence"?

What fascinated me wasn't just the comment- it was the assumption. The complete erasure of my agency, desire, pace, or humanity. As if my presence automatically implied consent. As if my interest in conversation was an open invitation.

And when I didn't respond with enthusiasm- when I instead responded with reality- the energy shifted.

Flaksters don't like mirrors.

They prefer surfaces.

Soon enough, he too faded. Another man allergic to emotional consequences and real repercussions may I say to their own actions. Another one who wanted access without presence, desire without depth, connection without containment.

Scene 3: S — The Confused Manipulator

(Or: The Man Who Mistook Emotional Labour for Foreplay)

S arrived softly.

No bravado. No crude innuendo. No obvious red flags flapping in the wind. He arrived instead with curiosity, time, and what appeared to be presence. The kind that feels rare in a distracted world.

There were all-night conversations- the kind that stretch past midnight and slip quietly into dawn. He asked questions. Deep ones. Childhood ones. Emotional ones. He said things like, "I really want to understand you." He listened in a way that felt intentional, almost reverent. He made space.

This is how the confused manipulator begins- not with lust, but with intimacy foreplay.

He mirrored. He leaned in. He cultivated closeness with the patience of someone watering a plant- slowly, attentively- until something in you softened and thought, Oh. This feels safe.

I was invested; it felt organic. Mutual. Earned. Not rushed.

And then I did the unthinkable.

I said I missed him.

Not dramatically. Not pleading. Just a simple statement- honest, unguarded, human.

That was the moment the atmosphere shifted.

Suddenly, he needed distance.

Suddenly, there was concern.

Suddenly, wisdom entered the chat.

"We will both get hurt if this continues," he said solemnly, as if delivering a spiritual truth instead of dodging accountability.

Translation: I've gotten what I wanted. Now I'm uncomfortable with the emotional consequences.

The pivot was so abrupt it could have caused whiplash. One moment, we were building connection brick by brick; the next, he was speaking in vague warnings, framing retreat as maturity.

This is the confused manipulator's speciality: turning withdrawal into virtue.

He didn't say, "I'm not available."

He said, "This is dangerous."

He didn't say, "I only wanted sex."

He said, "We're both getting too attached."

Notice the language. Always plural. Always mutual. Always just enough concern to sound ethical- never enough honesty to be accountable.

And then- like clockwork- he disappeared.

Not fully. Just enough. Enough silence to destabilise. Enough absence to make you question your perception. Enough distance to reset the power dynamic.

Months passed.

And because confused manipulators are not finished until the loop is complete, he circled back.

Casually. Lightly. As if time had erased context.

This time, however, he came with a revised narrative.

"Let's be honest," he said. "We both just wanted sex."

Ah. There it was.

The rewrite.

Suddenly, the all-night conversations weren't intimacy- they were foreplay. The emotional labour he so enthusiastically extracted was now reframed as mutual sexual interest. The investment I had made- carefully, consciously- was flattened into lust.

And then came the final sleight of hand.

He blamed me.

"You were only looking for sex," he said.

Which was truly a revelation- considering I was the one who expressed missing him, and he was the one who fled at the first sign of emotional continuity.

This is the masterstroke of the confused manipulator:

projecting his desire onto you, then punishing you for it.

By this point, the pattern was unmistakable.

- He created emotional closeness to gain access
- He withdrew when intimacy became real
- He reframed the connection to avoid responsibility
- He returned when he was lonely or horny
- He rewrote the story to absolve himself

And all of it was wrapped in confusion- his favourite camouflage.

Confused manipulators rarely appear predatory. They appear uncertain. Thoughtful. Afraid of hurting people. They use language that sounds self-aware while remaining deeply self-serving.

They are not confused.

They are conflict-avoidant opportunists.

They want the benefits of intimacy without the weight of it. They want access without relational consequences. They want to be wanted without being responsible for what wanting creates.

And when a woman names reality- when she says something as simple as "I miss you"- they retreat, not because it's too much, but because it exposes the imbalance.

What they cannot tolerate is being seen clearly.

The moment you stop playing along with the illusion- when you no longer accept the rewritten narrative- you step out of the fog.

And that is when the manipulation becomes obvious.

Because nothing reveals intent like consistency.

And nothing exposes a confused manipulator faster than a woman who refuses to accept confusion as truth.

The Feminism Excuse & the Provider Void

One of the most curious developments in modern dating is how selectively feminism is invoked.

Splitting the bill? Feminism.

Avoiding effort? Feminism.

No emotional labour? Feminism.

Yet somehow:

- Emotional availability is still expected from women

- Sexual openness is still assumed
- Caretaking is still silently outsourced

Equality has been weaponised to excuse absence, not partnership.

And let's be clear: providing is not just financial. It is energetic. Emotional. Attentive. Showing up. Waiting until she gets home. Remembering details. Creating safety.

Flaksters have abdicated even the smallest gestures of care- and then act shocked when women disengage.

Let's also address the strange economic theory some men seem to operate under: the Dinner-for-Sex Exchange Rate. Somewhere along the way, a few men appear to have concluded that if they pay for a meal, they have effectively purchased access to a woman's body.

I'm sorry, sir — did buying me pasta come with a subscription plan to my physical intimacy that I somehow missed the memo on?

Yes, paying the bill does send a signal. But the signal is not "Congratulations, you've unlocked Level Two." What it actually signals is something far simpler: that you are generous, reasonably stable, and capable of managing the basic logistics of adult life — such as covering dinner without requiring a repayment plan.

That is the signal.

It is not a receipt.

It is not a down payment.

And it is certainly not a coupon redeemable for access to my body.

If buying someone a meal automatically entitled you to sex, restaurants would have to start printing "consent included" on the menu — somewhere between the garlic bread and the tiramisu.

A woman is checking for security and stability and a man paying the bill on a date communicates just that.

The Core Pattern

The Flakster is driven by temporary newness.

Once depth appears, once intimacy becomes real- once a woman reveals that she is not a recreational activity but a sovereign being- the Flakster panics.

Because real intimacy requires:

- Self-reflection
- Consistency
- Responsibility
- And above all- Presence

And Flaksters are not here for growth.

They are here for stimulation.

So, they disappear.

Then return.

Then disappear again.

Not because you are "too much."

But because you are real.

The Quiet Truth

The tragedy is not that these men exist.

The tragedy is how normalised this behaviour has become.

Women begin doubting themselves for wanting:

- Consistency
- Safety
- Basic respect

They are told to "relax," "be chill," "not overthink."

But here is the truth Flaksters don't want you to see:

Wanting clarity is not being clingy or needing too much; that's the bare minimum, ladies.

Wanting effort is not demanding.

Wanting respect is not old-fashioned, again bare minimum.

It is sane.

And the moment you stop auditioning for men who treat dating like a hobby, you step out of the trap entirely.

Because you are not a hitchhiker.

You are not a pit stop.

And you are certainly not a detour on someone's way to nowhere.

The Spiritual Trap

Flaky men often trigger something deeper:

Your wounded feminine- the part of you that is still seeking external validation, safety, or worth.

They come into your life not to love you, but to show you where you haven't loved yourself yet.

And until you learn that lesson, the Universe keeps sending you the same energy in different bodies.

It's a loop. A karmic classroom.

A Field Guide to Spotting the Flakster Early

Flaksters are not subtle once you know the signs.

Behavioural markers include:

- Early sexual comments without emotional context
- "Go with the flow" as a lifestyle philosophy
- Aversion to labels, clarity, or timelines, and I see so many of my lady friends getting brain-washed into thinking this was their idea.
- Discomfort when emotions enter the room
- Charm without follow-through, no action, just talks
- Selective feminism (used to avoid effort)
- Disappearing when depth emerges, reappearing when things are convenient and yes, to meet their needs and erase yours

They are deeply invested in optionality- keeping doors open, women interchangeable, and accountability minimal.

They want:

- Your body
- Your attention
- Your emotional availability

But not:

- Your expectations
- Your needs
- Your reality

And here stands the crucial truth women must internalise:

A man who wants you in fragments does not secretly want you whole.

No amount of patience, sensuality, understanding, or spiritual maturity will convert a Flakster into a partner. He is not unfinished- he is choosing avoidance.

Why Women Keep Engaging (And Why It Hurts)

Many women say they don't want situationships- yet keep entering them.

Why?

Because situationships often feel easier at first. They offer attention without confrontation, connection without commitment, desire without decision. For women healing from abandonment, rejection, or emotional deprivation, this can feel soothing- temporarily. They settle because they innately feel that's all that they are worth. But don't realise that these are simply emotional whirlwinds and rollercoasters that, with time, will fray their nervous system and lead to heartbreak.

If you are engaging in situationships hoping they will become relationships, you are already betraying yourself.

Situationships are not neutral. They are not "undefined" by accident. They are defined by avoidance.

Women who truly do not want this dynamic must stop participating in it- not by convincing men to change, but by withdrawing consent from structures that harm them.

Ask yourself:

- Am I engaging because this aligns with my values, or because I fear being alone?
- Am I hoping proximity will create commitment?
- Am I silencing my needs to stay connected?

If the answer is yes, the cost will come due.

Because the longer you remain in emotional limbo, the more your nervous system adapts to instability. Inconsistency begins to feel normal. Waiting becomes a habit. Hope becomes a leash.

Flaksters thrive on this.

Recalibration: Choosing Out of the Flakster Economy

Here is the hard truth that sets women free:

You must opt out of the modern dating chaos.

Do not protest it.

Do not negotiate with it.

Do not endure it better.

Opt out.

This means:

- Saying no to ambiguity
- Ending connections that lack direction early
- Refusing sexual access without emotional safety
- Trusting disinterest as information
- Walking away the first time you feel reduced

You are not old-fashioned for wanting consistency.

You are not demanding for wanting clarity.

You are not broken for wanting depth.

You are simply not compatible with men who want to sample life without committing to it.

And here is the quiet recalibration women must make:

Stop treating attention as interest.

Stop treating charm as character.

A man who wants a partner will not confuse you.

A man who values you will not keep you guessing.

A man who is capable of intimacy will not run from it.

The Flakster Pattern Self-Check

(Am I Dealing with a Flakster—or Avoiding the Truth?)

1. Is clarity consistently avoided?
    - Do conversations about direction, intentions, or exclusivity get redirected, joked away, or delayed?

    Avoidance of clarity is not confusion- it is a strategy.
2. Does the connection intensify physically faster than it deepens emotionally?
    - Are sexual comments, innuendos, or access prioritised before trust, safety, or emotional attunement?

    When desire outruns presence, you are being consumed- not chosen.
3. Do his words and actions frequently misalign?
    - Is he warm in conversation but inconsistent in showing up?

    Charm without continuity is a Flakster signature.
4. Does he frame expectations as pressure?
    - Are your needs described as "too much," "heavy," or "complicating things"?

    Pathologising your needs protects his avoidance.
5. Are you doing all the emotional labour without any relational security?
    - Do you listen, soothe, support, or emotionally invest without knowing where you stand?

    Care without containment drains you.
6. Does he disappear when things feel real- and reappear when it feels easy?
    - Is there a pattern of withdrawal after intimacy or depth?

    This is not timing. It is emotional unavailability.
7. Are you staying because of potential rather than reality? This is a big one. Women fall for the potential all the time.

   - Are you hoping consistency will emerge later?

   Potential is not a relationship. It is a story you tell yourself.

8. Are you tolerating ambiguity you wouldn't recommend to another woman?
   - Would you advise a friend to stay in this dynamic?

   Your standards are already speaking.

9. Does being with him activate anxiety more than safety?
   - Do you overthink texts, timing, or tone?

   A regulated connection does not keep you guessing.

10. If nothing changed, would this dynamic still meet your emotional needs?
    - Imagine six months or a year of this exact pattern. Your body's response is your answer.

How to Read Your Answers

- 2–3 "yes" responses: Pause and observe closely.
- 4–6 "yes" responses: You are likely engaging a Flakster pattern.
- 7 or more "yes" responses: This dynamic is already costing you emotionally.

If you want stability, stop dating men who want freedom at your expense.

Your nervous system knows before your mind admits it.

Leaving the Roadside

Flaksters are not villains. They are symptoms of a culture that rewards avoidance, celebrates detachment, and eroticises non-commitment.

But you do not have to participate.

You are not here to teach grown men how to treat women.

When you stop engaging with men who want fragments of you, something radical happens: your nervous system calms. The craving for intensity dissolves. The addiction to anticipation fades.

And suddenly, what once felt exciting now feels exhausting.

That is growth.

Not louder boundaries.

No better explanations.

Just choosing differently.

Because the moment you leave the roadside, you stop meeting men who are only passing through.

Breaking the Pattern: Zero Tolerance

This cycle only ends when you decide it ends.

When you:

- Raise your standards.
- Stop getting charmed by words.
- Contain your energy. Flaksters are attracted to the search energy much like moths to a flame. Searching for "The Twin Flame" in every man you meet will definitely put you right in this trap.
- Observe consistency instead of chemistry.
- Ask: "Is there a label? - or am I being manipulated and cajoled into believing that I don't need one."

- Ask: "Are they integrating me into their life or am I simply a bedroom prop?"
- Ask: "Is this relationship expanding my sense of self or shrinking it, even erasing it?"
- Are there efforts and actions being taken, or is it just false and hollow promises

If you're only present in their bedroom and not their world... that's not a relationship.

That's a convenient arrangement- one that is masterfully designed by him.

We live in a swipe-left, swipe-right culture where people treat humans like temporary entertainment. The world is designed to keep everyone in a loop of novelty, not depth.

So how do you become someone's destination in a culture addicted to detours?

You stop trying.

Because the real truth is this:

When you become your own destination, only then can someone else treat you like one.

Flakiness dissolves when your boundaries solidify.

Manipulators disappear when your intuition sharpens.

Half lovers fall away when your self-love becomes non-negotiable.

You are not here to perform for love.

You are here to embody it.

And when you do, the universe stops sending you lessons.

It starts sending you matches. Not from Tinder but from Destiny.

The Flakster First-Date Filter

First, I will say this is not your fault.

The current dating market is genuinely saturated with Flaksters- men optimised for novelty, stimulation, and temporary connection. What looks like abundance is often an illusion. You are not "choosing wrong." You are navigating a culture that rewards emotional minimalism and sexual access without responsibility.

The pattern usually goes like this:

- 48 hours of intense chemistry
- Rapid escalation
- A sense of "Wow, this feels different"
- Physical intimacy
- Poof. He vanishes like a ghost with Wi-Fi issues

And later—once loneliness or boredom strikes- you receive the midnight "Hey baby" text. Not because he misses you, but because his bed is cold and his ego needs warming.

This is not intimacy.

This is a revolving door with better lighting.

Now- onto the filter.

The First-Date Filter

1. **Does he ask why you're dating—or just what you're into?**
    - Is he curious about your values, life, and direction?
    - Or does the conversation drift quickly toward bodies, vibes, and "energy"?

    Flaksters want access, not context.
2. **How does he handle the bill, show chivalry and take care while making small efforts?**

    This isn't about money- it's about orientation.
    - Does he naturally offer and handle it with ease?
    - Or does he awkwardly freeze, invoke feminism, or act like paying for coffee is a political stance?
    - Does he give you a more comfortable seat at the cafe?
    - Does he make sure you get home safe?

    Effort shows up in small moments first.
3. **Does sexual commentary arrive suspiciously early?**
    - Is he already "joking" about sex on date one or two?
    - Framing it as confidence, honesty, or "just being open"?

    Early sexualisation is not boldness- it is entitlement wearing cologne.
4. **Does he leave you with continuity- or just chemistry?**
    - Does he check in after the date?
    - Make a clear plan to see you again?

    A man who is serious does not leave you floating. Period.
5. **How does he talk about relationships?**

    Listen closely.
    - "I'm open but not looking to settle."
    - "Let's see where it goes."
    - "I don't want to label things."

Translation: I want the benefits without any responsibility.

6. **Does he disappear after closeness?**

   If intimacy- emotional or physical-is followed by sudden distance, delays, or vagueness…

   That's not timing. That's a Flakster retreating once his needs are met.

7. **Are you already adjusting yourself?**
   - Softening your needs?
   - Laughing off discomfort?
   - Telling yourself to "be chill"?

   The moment you self-edit to stay connected, you're no longer dating- you're negotiating with your own self-worth.

8. **Does he treat your presence like a privilege—or a convenience?**
   - Planned dates vs last-minute pings
   - Daylight invitations vs midnight nostalgia

   Booty calls are not affection. They are loneliness management.

9. **How does your body feel after the date?**
   - Calm?
   - Clear?
   - Or anxious, buzzing, and overthinking?

   Chemistry without safety is just adrenaline.

10. **If this exact pattern continued for three months, would you feel nourished- or depleted?**

    Don't imagine change.

    Imagine consistency. Your answer is your truth.

The Hard but Liberating Truth

If you do not want situationships, stop engaging in situationship behaviour.

That means:

- No sexual access without emotional clarity
- No "seeing where it goes" when you know where you want to go
- No waiting for men to choose you after you've already chosen yourself

Flaksters thrive because women are socialised to be understanding, flexible, and patient. But clarity does not kill connection- it filters out people who were never aligned.

Closing Note: About the Ghosting

When a Flakster vanishes after intensity, it is not because you were too much.

It's because:

- Depth makes him uncomfortable
- Presence requires effort
- Intimacy demands maturity

And when he resurfaces at 11:47 PM with "You up?"—remember:

You are not a late-night service.

You are not a comfort object.

You are not a warming device for a man avoiding his own life.

The real thing does not feel confusing.

It does not disappear after closeness.

It does not require you to shrink.

The Flaksters are loud, visible, and plentiful- but they are not the standard.

And the moment you apply this filter, you stop meeting ghosts- and start meeting men who can actually stay.

The Flaksters Detox

How to Exit the Cycle, Reset Your Nervous System, and Reclaim Your Standards

Flaksters fatigue is real.

It is the weariness of false starts, emotional whiplash, and conversations that go nowhere but somehow still drain everything.

If you feel tired, cynical, numb, or over it, you are not broken. You are overstimulated by inconsistency.

This is not a personal failing. It is a systemic pattern in the modern dating market. But healing does not come from explaining yourself better or filtering harder alone- it comes from detoxing.

This section is not about becoming "less attached."

It is about becoming more sovereign.

Step 1: Name the Fatigue Without Blaming Yourself

The first layer of detox is relief.

Say this clearly:

"I am not unlucky. I am navigating a dating culture that rewards flakiness and penalises depth."

Repeated exposure to Flaksters trains the nervous system to expect disappearance after connection. Over time, women internalise this as self-doubt:

- Maybe I'm too intense.
- Maybe I ask for too much.
- Maybe this is just how dating is now.

It isn't.

You are not failing at dating- you are responding normally to abnormal conditions.

The fatigue you feel is not emotional weakness. It is your system asking for rest from unpredictability.

Step 2: Enforce a No-Ambiguity Cleanse

Detox requires boundaries- not as punishments, but as protections.

For a set period (30–90 days is ideal), commit to this rule:

No dating dynamics that lack clarity, continuity, or conscious intention.

This means:

- No "let's see where it goes"
- No late-night texts as connection
- No situationships you hope will evolve

- No emotional labour without emotional security

This is not about making demands.

It is about withdrawing access from structures that exhaust you.

Flaksters rely on ambiguity to survive. The moment clarity is required; they opt out- saving you time, energy, and attachment.

Step 3: Reset the Nervous System (This Is Non-Negotiable)

Flaksters fatigue is not just emotional- it is physiological.

Inconsistent connection creates:

- Hypervigilance
- Dopamine spikes followed by crashes
- Anxiety mistaken for chemistry
- Waiting patterns in the body

To detox, the body must learn safety again.

Prioritise:

- Regular sleep
- Gentle movement (walking, stretching, yoga)
- Touch that is non-sexual and safe
- Time without dating apps or romantic pursuit

Notice how your body responds when:

- No one is disappearing
- No one is confusing you
- No one is dangling attention

At first, the quiet may feel unsettling. That is withdrawal- not loneliness.

Stay with it.

Step 4: Break the Intensity Addiction

Many women exiting Flakster patterns realise something uncomfortable:

They became addicted to intensity.

Not because they are dramatic- but because inconsistency trains the brain to chase relief. The spike of attention feels euphoric precisely because it is unpredictable.

Detox means redefining attraction.

Ask yourself:

- Does this person bring peace- or adrenaline?
- Do I feel more myself- or more anxious and small?
- Am I expanding- or bracing?

Healthy attraction is often quieter at first. It builds steadily. It does not hijack your nervous system.

If something feels too electric early on, pause. Let time do the screening.

Step 5: Reclaim Desire Without Access

One of the most empowering parts of detox is separating desire from availability.

You are allowed to:

- Want intimacy
- Enjoy the attraction
- Feel sensual

Without:

- Acting on it immediately
- Trading access for attention
- Offering your body as proof of connection

Flaksters confuse sexual access with intimacy. Detox teaches you that desire does not obligate you to perform it. Sensuality can look like adorning and admiring the self without the presence of a man, especially a flaky one.

Step 6: Reorient Toward Full-Life Nourishment

Flaksters fatigue narrows life. Everything starts orbiting around:

- Texts
- Responses
- Availability
- Potential

Detox widens the field.

Refill your life with:

- Reciprocal Friendships
- Work that engages you
- Creativity that absorbs you
- Rituals that anchor you

The less your nervous system depends on romantic stimulation for aliveness, the less power Flaksters have over you.

Step 7: Upgrade Your Internal Standard

The final layer of detox is internal- not external.

Move from:

"Does he like me?"

to

"Do I feel safe, seen, heard and steady here?"

Your body is now the authority.

If:

- You feel confused → pause
- You feel anxious → slow down
- You feel diminished → disengage

You no longer need closure, explanation, or confirmation.

Your experience is enough.

Closing: Leaving the Flaksters Era

Flaksters fatigue ends the moment you stop negotiating with confusion.

You do not need thicker skin.

You do not need better flirting skills.

You do not need to try harder.

You need less access to what drains you and more allegiance to what sustains you.

The dating market may still be crowded with Flaksters- but you no longer have to meet them.

When you detox:

- Your nervous system resets
- Your standards clarify
- Your attraction recalibrates

And what once felt exciting now feels empty.

That is not loss.

That is discernment.

The real thing does not exhaust you.

It does not vanish.

It does not require you to abandon yourself.

And once your system remembers that, you stop settling for ghosts altogether.

CHAPTER 3

THE CYBER-SCAM MAN TRAP

It was the middle of the pandemic.

The world had stopped spinning.

But inside me, everything was spiralling- loneliness, restlessness, hunger for connection, for meaning, for a sign that love was not done with me yet.

That's when the DM came.

A random "psychic" on Instagram- profile full of crystals, celestial symbols, and generic spiritual quotes, but hardly any followers.

She messaged me like she had been waiting for me specifically.

"You are a rare soul."

"You're meant for divine union."

"Your true soulmate is your first love."

And I fell for it.

Not because I was foolish.

But because I was hungry- hungry for belonging,

hungry for a love story that would finally make sense of all my heartbreaks.

So, when she said my "true home" was with my first boyfriend- let's call him P- something in me softened.

It took me back to a younger version of myself who believed in destiny, in first love magic, in reincarnation romance.

So, I reached out to him.

And that was the beginning of one of the strangest, most disturbing man-traps of my life.

P- The Charm Artist with Empty Eyes and Expensive Desires

Let me describe P.

He had always been money-minded.

Even in our younger days, he was transactional in ways that made my intuition cringe out of its seat. He would desire only branded watches and t-shirts, which, let me add, were all out of his reach.

But charm?

He had that mastered.

Smooth, easy, boyish in the right places, worldly in others- a perfect mix of nostalgia and seduction.

So, when we reconnected during the lockdown, he played the part with precision.

Hours of conversations.

Laughing about old memories.

Romanticising the longing. Even calling me his wife!

Painting a picture of "maybe we were always meant to come back."

He knew exactly which emotional strings to pull.

But this time, it wasn't money he was after.

It was something darker.

Something kinkier.

Something he thought he could rope me into under the pretext of destiny.

The Fetish Reveal

It started subtly.

A mention of experimentation.

A hint about fantasy and fetishes.

A casual comment about "modern relationships."

Then he dropped the bomb:

"I've always wanted a threesome."

Not as a curiosity, but as a fixation.

He said it with the entitlement of someone discussing lunch, like this was a natural progression of our "soulmate reunion."

I was stunned.

This was not the language of love.

This was not a reunion of hearts.

This was a man trying to slot me into his sexual bucket list.

But the real nightmare hadn't even begun.

The Psychic Returned- And This Time, she was after my friends

The same Instagram psychic suddenly messaged my female friends.

All the vulnerable ones.

Almost in a pattern.

Her pitch?

"You are meant to join Kalashree and P in a sacred sexual union."

"A divine threesome will unlock your energies and align your chakras towards enlightenment." The way these masqueraders humiliate spirituality fails to astound me.

I remember staring at my phone, heart pounding, bile rising.

It wasn't spiritual guidance- it was coordinated grooming.

And that's when everything in me snapped.

The Investigation

Anger has a clarity that fear doesn't.

I traced the pattern of messages.

The timing.

The language.

The weird overlaps.

The emotional manipulation felt identical to the way P spoke.

So, I got the IP address checked.

And the truth was worse than I imagined.

The psychic…

was P.

The man was running a two-person scam.

He had crafted a fake account to lure me.

Then used the same account to lure my friends into his sexual fantasies.

He was literally catfishing women into fulfilling his fetish-

using spirituality as bait.

Using "soulmate destiny" as a trap.

And I was done.

I blocked him everywhere.

I cut the psychic (him) off.

I told my friends the truth.

I walked away with my dignity intact, even if my faith in humanity cracked immensely and eroded at my trusting and open heart.

His Patterns- His Shadows

P was not complicated.

He was predictable:

- Narcissistic need for attention
- Manipulation disguised as spirituality
- Sexual opportunism
- Charm deployed like a weapon
- Lack of accountability
- Fetish-driven obsession
- Delusion packaged as destiny
- Ensnaring and conning emotionally vulnerable women
- Using their love as their weakness to gain at their expense

He wasn't looking for love.

He was looking for access.

And he was willing to deceive, impersonate, and violate boundaries to get it.

My Patterns

And if I'm being honest?

I attracted this because:

- I wanted a soulmate so badly, I ignored my instincts. This Man Trap was the big one that helped me dismantle my Twin Flame longing. I realised deeply and unwaveringly that this desire of mine was landing me in nothing but trouble. The deeper I went down this road, the harsher the lessons were becoming in the guise of increasingly toxic men
- My abandonment wound was louder than my intuition
- I still associated "first love" with safety
- I wanted magic during a dark and isolating time
- The loneliness of the lockdown made illusions look like signs of destined love

It wasn't stupidity. It was longing. And longing makes prey out of even the strongest women.

Message to the Reader

Protect Your Heart in the Digital Age. The cyber-scam man trap is spreading- because it works.

During isolation, during heartbreak, during longing…

Women are more vulnerable to digital seduction.

Predators know this.

They wrap manipulation in:

- spirituality
- soulmate rhetoric
- destiny stories
- divination quotes
- "Twin flame" nonsense

- fake psychic accounts

And before you know it, you're trapped in a psychological web designed by a man who sees you as a supply, not a soul.

Here's what I want every reader to know:

- Never trust anyone who uses "spiritual guidance" to interfere with your romantic choices.
- A soulmate will NEVER need a psychic to announce his arrival.
- Any man who tries to sexualise you through a third party is dangerous.
- Charm is easy. Integrity is rare.
- Your loneliness is not an invitation for predators.
- Your intuition is far more accurate than any psychic on Instagram.

And most importantly:

If a man needs to pretend to be someone else just to access your body…

He was never a soulmate.

He was a warning.

The Core Patterns in Women That Attract Sexual Fantasies Masquerading as Love

(This is not an indictment. It is a map.)

Let's say this clearly first:

Predators are responsible for predation. Period.

However, awareness of these scams is powerful. Certain inner configurations- especially during times of isolation, grief, transition, or spiritual openness- can act like open Wi-Fi signals to men who are hunting for access, not intimacy.

Here are seven core patterns that cyber-scam men exploit with surgical precision.

1. The Soulmate Hunger Pattern

This is NOT romanticism.

This is unmet attachment longing wearing spiritual language.

Women with this pattern:

- Want love to mean something cosmic or karmic
- Feel tired of "randomness" in dating
- Want one story that redeems all the pain before it

Predators use destiny language because it bypasses discernment and goes straight to hope. Hope is the biggest pitfall of an open heart. "Perhaps he might be the one syndrome."

2. The Spiritual Bypass Pattern

When spiritual frameworks are used to override emotional red flags.

Signs:

- "Maybe this is a karmic lesson" I have heard this countless times, even in my own friend circle, and I have been guilty of this one many times over
- "Spiritual love transcends boundaries"

This is where manipulation thrives- because anything can be reframed as "growth."

3. The First-Love Imprint Pattern

First love lives in the nervous system, not just memory.

For many women:

- First love equals safety, innocence, before-damage
- Reconnecting feels like reclaiming a lost self

Predators exploit this by reactivating nostalgia to bypass present-day standards.

4. The Healer Identity Pattern

Women who:

- Hold space easily
- See potential instead of behaviour- women do this all the time, we fall for the hypothetical man- the projected fantasy, not the reality of the scum that is before us
- Believe love can awaken men

Sexual opportunists know healers often delay boundaries "until clarity emerges."

5. The Loneliness- During-Transition Pattern

Lockdowns. Breakups. Career pauses. Spiritual awakenings. Relocations.

During liminal phases:

- The psyche is more susceptible
- Signs feel louder

- Attention feels like a drug

Predators don't arrive when you're stable. They arrive when you're between selves.

6. The Validation Scarcity Pattern

Not low self-esteem- but long stretches without relational mirroring.

This creates:

- Over-investment in anyone who "sees" you
- Difficulty stepping back once intimacy begins

Predators escalate fast to secure emotional real estate early.

7. The "Open-Minded Woman" Trap

Sexual progressiveness weaponised against women.

Used phrases:

- "You're evolved"
- "You're not like other women"

What's actually happening:

Your boundaries are being framed as limitations, and your openness is being used as an invitation for anything goes behaviour.

The Cyber-Scam Man Trap: A 10-Question Reality-Check Checklist

Before emotional, spiritual, or sexual engagement deepens, ask yourself—slowly, honestly—these ten questions:

1. **Does this connection require secrecy, urgency, or specialness?**
   Healthy love expands your life.
   Scams compress it.
2. **Is spirituality being used to justify boundary-crossing?**
   Spiritual language should support consent, not dissolve it.
3. **Does he sexualize the connection before safety is established?**
   Intimacy follows trust, not the other way around!
   Objectification precedes extraction and exploitation.
4. **Is he outsourcing accountability to "energies," "fate," or "higher guidance"?**
   Men who cannot own desire hide behind metaphysics.
5. **Are third parties being introduced to manage or escalate intimacy?**
   Any sexual triangulation without explicit, grounded consent is a red flag.
6. **Does your nervous system feel calmer—or more activated?**
   Anxiety is not passion.
   Confusion is not chemistry. I cannot repeat this one enough.
7. **Is he curious about your inner world—or focused on your availability?**
   Interest in access is not interest in you.
8. **Are your instincts being reframed as fear, ego, or trauma?**
   Your intuition does not need healing—it needs listening.
9. **Does he disappear, shift tone, or deflect when you ask direct questions?**
   Truth withstands clarity.

Manipulation avoids it.

10. **If a friend told you this story, what would you advise her?**

    Your wisdom exists. Use it on yourself.

    If more than three questions raise discomfort, pause immediately.

    No soulmate evaporates under scrutiny.

    Only illusory ghosts do.

Releasing, Detoxing, and Reclaiming Sovereignty After Violation

(How to heal without shattering your heart and eroding your soul)

The aftermath of a cyber-scam man trap isn't just disappointment.

It is a massive violation. Violation of trust. Violation of consent.

Violation of basic safety. Violation of the sacred inner terrain where desire meets dignity.

The shame that follows is not yours to carry—but it must be metabolised.

Step 1: Name What Happened—Without Self-Blame

You were manipulated, not "naïve." Your friends might even call you foolish or naive. Do not internalise this judgement.

You were targeted, not careless.

Predators succeed by:

- Mimicking intimacy
- Studying vulnerabilities like patterns

- Exploiting timing

Naming the truth restores cognitive authority.

Step 2: Grieve the Illusion, Not the Man

You are not grieving him.

You are grieving:

- The hope
- The meaning
- The story you were briefly allowed to believe

Let that grief move.

Unexpressed grief calcifies into self-doubt, ultimately deepening the heart wound.

Step 3: Detox the Fantasy Loop

Fantasy is where predators linger longest.

Practices:

- Write down the facts only (not intentions, not potential)
- Break the "what if" narrative
- Reclaim reality as grounding medicine

Reality is not cruel. Reality is protective. It is your agency.

Step 4: Restore the Body's Authority

Violation disconnects women from their bodies.

Reconnection practices:

- Grounded movement
- Breath anchored in the lower body
- Touch that is self-directed, not performative
- Reclaiming your energy by repeating "this is not my fault"

Your body is not an offering.

It is a sacred home.

Step 5: Rebuild Discernment as a Skill, not a Trait

Discernment is not instinct alone—it is trained perception.

Reclaim it by:

- Slowing emotional escalation
- Observing consistency over charm
- Tracking behaviour, not words

This is not cynicism.

It is maturity.

Step 6: Re-Establish Sexual Sovereignty

Being objectified fractures erotic self-trust.

Reclamation means:

- Redefining desire on your terms
- Decoupling sex from approval
- Knowing that access is earned, not granted

Your desire is sacred. Not negotiable.

Step 7: Close the Energetic Door

Energetic closure matters—even without belief systems.

Ritualise the ending:

- Write what you are releasing. Write a strong letter to the reality of the man who paraded love before you. Let the facade of the man go.
- State aloud what is no longer permitted
- Affirm boundaries as law, not preference

The psyche responds to ceremony.

Step 8: Replace Self-Judgment with Self-Respect

Shame keeps predators alive in memory. We often blame ourselves for being misled. This is self-gaslighting and does grave harm. Healing occurs when we let ourselves off the hook. Remembering we are not the perpetrators. Releasing the shame and guilt.

Instead say:

"I survived manipulation with awareness intact."

"I protected myself when clarity arrived."

"I chose dignity over fantasy."

That is strength.

Step 9: Install New Filters

Going forward, your filters are:

- Emotional transparency

- Behavioural consistency
- Respect for pace
- Absence of spiritual coercion

Anyone offended by your boundaries was never meant to stay.

Step 10: Reclaim the Heart—Without Closing It

The goal is not hardness.

The goal is precision. Discernment.

A heart with boundaries is not closed.

It is sovereign.

Final Truth

You were not reduced. You were tested.

And you emerged:

- Clearer
- Stronger
- Less available to illusion
- More aligned with your own authority

Any man who needs deception to access you

was never your destiny.

He was the final lesson

before you remembered who you are.

CHAPTER 4

THE SEXUAL ABUSE MAN TRAP

The Sexual Abuse Man Trap is one of the most insidious of them all, because it doesn't always arrive with a knife in the dark. Sometimes it comes wearing beads and chanting mantras. Sometimes it comes cloaked in "consciousness," speaking the language of healing and spirituality while hiding a predatory hunger beneath the robe.

Let's call him H.

He found me through a work call- yes, a work call- for the global conscious community I was leading communications for. A movement with 500+ organisations dedicated to healing, farming, sustainability, and planetary well-being. A place where integrity was meant to be sacred. And yet, at the top of this ecosystem stood a thirty-year-old man whose soul was darker than the shadows he pretended to work against.

The moment he saw me on screen, I felt it-that latch.

A psychic hook.

A predatory claim masked as "connection."

He began pursuing me under the guise of spiritual invitations- Yatras, journeys, and pilgrimages for which he had zero training, depth, or alignment to lead. When I refused, he pushed harder, the way emotionally underdeveloped men do- tantruming toddlers in grown bodies who cannot tolerate a woman's autonomy.

When I still declined, he shifted tactics.

Charm.

Promises.

Talks of marriage.

The illusion of emotional depth.

I went to Udaipur for work-related reasons; he made it about access. I was clear about my boundaries. I said I needed time. I said I was not ready for physical intimacy. But predators do not seek consent- they seek weakness, gaps, trauma, and the quiet corners where a woman's unhealed inner child still freezes.

And freeze is exactly what my inner child did. Instead of my autonomous-self taking over, my unhealed and scared inner child did.

What followed was not intimacy. It was coercion dressed as closeness. Manipulation disguised as affection. A man using spiritual language and incessant emotional pressure to override my agency.

And because trauma recognition is not instant, because survival fawning is a real response, because childhood wounds echo into adulthood- I endured what I should have walked away from.

But back then, the empowered woman in me was buried under layers of unhealed pain. The girl who had been shamed into silence as a child rose to the surface. And he sensed that. Predators always do.

When I returned home, it did not end. He stalked me virtually, hiding behind the shield of work. He harassed me after team calls, imposing himself through private video calls, violating boundaries again and again. This psychological and sexualized pressure began manifesting in my body- hours and hours of intense pelvic pain, hormonal imbalance, bleeding, anxiety, shame, guilt. Trauma always finds a physical doorway.

And when I told my parents, hoping for protection, I was met with silence, slut- shaming, fear, and dismissal. When I finally spoke to my boss- the very leader of this "conscious" community- he gaslit me and retorted that I had "more experience" and should "know how to handle men."

Imagine that- my pain brushed aside to protect his surrogate son H.

This is how predators thrive- not alone, but supported by enablers, cowards, and men who refuse to hold other men accountable.

Then came the breaking point.

I snapped.

Or rather, Kali snapped through me.

The force that rises when a woman has been pushed too far. The rage that is not destructive but purifying. The voice that roars when silence has become poison.

I voiced a three-hour-long complaint to the global community. Not a cry for help- an indictment. A testimony. A reckoning.

And suddenly, truth had consequences.

H was removed.

Investigations opened.

Multiple survivors came forward.

Stories emerged of him targeting women across ages, races, and geographies. He nearly drowned a teenage girl who rejected his advances. A pattern emerged, which was so clear it could no longer be smothered under Sanskrit chants and spirituality theatrics.

The entire structure trembled.

But this chapter isn't about him.

It's about recognising the trap before you fall into it.

The Sexual Abuse Man Trap operates on confusion.

"Did I want this?"

"Did I invite it?"

"Was it assault or did I somehow consent?"

Predators rely on that disorientation.

On your self-doubt.

On your wounded inner child.

On your longing for love, connection, mentorship, or belonging.

So, here is the ultimate takeaway, the one that every girl, every woman, every feminine being needs etched into her bones:

"If you have to convince yourself it's okay, it is

Not okay.

If you feel pressured, confused, or guilty, it is not consent.

If he claims love but ignores your boundaries, it is not love."

True love waits for readiness.

True masculinity honours boundaries.

True spirituality never manipulates.

He was not a man—he was a monster who frankly belongs behind bars because such men can never reform.

A dark lesson. A succubus whose sole intention was to feed off the light of others.

A soul whose presence teaches women to trust the voice inside them long before they trust the words outside them.

And that is where liberation begins.

H's biggest shadow was that he was a predator in all forms possible. He was someone who could sap a woman dry to the point of being lifeless. He could drain her mind, body and soul, all of her resources until she was nothing but a hollow shell of the person she once was. And that is the epitome of someone whose darkness is a void- so deep that it can engulf another. This person doesn't have shadow patterns-NO- he is the shadow himself. He simply ignored the word "NO." This, in turn, was my greatest test in reclaiming my power, my voice, and ultimately my truth.

And women don't attract these predators. These predators simply exist where patriarchy, unsafety and misogyny are rampant. In all my travels, the truth is that only in India have I come across this particular man trap where the word NO is just not in the man's vocabulary. No wonder we are the rape capital of the world. This level of entitlement, where the other has zero agency, is stark, shocking and inhumane. This is NOT a test of your boundaries. Let's be logical here. When a man doesn't take no for an answer, how can boundaries be the solution when they are being totally bulldozed over? The only thing to do is to get as far away from such a man as possible because safety is just not in their DNA.

A Somatic & Boundary Pattern Recognition Test

This test is to help you recognise predatory behaviour early on. You do not need to score all 10.

Two or three is already a warning.

1. **Body Before Thought Test**
   Question: What does your body do before your mind forms an opinion?
   Check for:
   - Sudden freezing

- Tight throat or jaw
- Pelvic clenching
- Shallow breath
- A feeling of being "hooked" or claimed

Red flag: If your body contracts before your mind tries to explain it away. The body registers threat faster than language.

2. **Speed & Pressure Test**

Question: Does he accelerate intimacy—emotional, spiritual, or sexual—before trust has been built?

Check for:

- Fast bonding
- Premature "specialness"
- Urgency disguised as destiny
- Pressure framed as passion or truth

Red flag: If "now" is more important to him than your readiness.

3. **Boundary Response Test**

Set one clear, calm boundary. Then observe.

Healthy response looks like:

- Acceptance
- Space
- No emotional penalty

Predatory response looks like:

- Sulking
- Persuasion
- Guilt
- Spiritual reframing ("You're blocked / afraid / resisting love")

Boundaries do not require explanation. Resistance to them reveals character. Predators do not take NO for an answer. They rely on coercion and detect vulnerability as prey.

4. **Language–Behaviour Mismatch Test**

   Question: Do his words and actions align?

   Check for:

   - "Conscious" language with coercive behaviour
   - Claims of love with disregard for consent
   - Spiritual talk paired with entitlement

   Red flag: If his vocabulary has evolved but his nervous system has not.

5. **Confusion Loop Test**

   Question: Do you find yourself repeatedly asking:

   - "Did I want this?"
   - "Was it my fault?"
   - "Am I overreacting?"

   Red flag: Confusion after interaction is not chemistry—it is disorientation.

   Clarity is a sign of safety.

   Confusion is a sign of violation.

6. **Isolation Drift Test**

   Question: Do you feel subtly pulled away from:

   - Friends
   - Mentors
   - Support systems
   - Your own inner authority

   Red flag: If he positions himself as the primary interpreter of your experience. This is a huge red flag; predators thrive on isolation- on becoming the centre of your universe. This also helps them in more than one way- one, you become more dependent on them, and two, you cannot verify their patterns with other common connections, leaving you completely at their disposal.

7. **Inner Child Activation Test**

   Notice: Do you feel younger around him?

   Check for:

   - People-pleasing
   - Freezing
   - Fear of displeasing
   - Loss of adult agency

   Red flag: Predators target the child state, not the sovereign adult.

8. **After-Effect Test**

   After interacting with him, do you feel:

   - Drained
   - Ashamed
   - Anxious
   - Disconnected from your body
   - Physically unwell

   Red flag: If your body pays a price for his presence. Trauma always leaves a somatic footprint.

9. **Accountability Test**

   Question: When confronted, does he:

   - Take responsibility

   OR

   - Deflect, gaslight, spiritualise, or blame?

   Red flag: A man who cannot hold accountability will never hold consent.

10. **Truth Simplicity Test (The Final Gate)**
    Ask yourself one question—slowly, honestly:
    "If I remove all explanations, does this feel safe?"
    If the answer is no, that is your answer.

The Rule to Etch into the Nervous System

If you have to convince yourself it's okay, it is not okay.

If there is pressure, it is not consent.

If boundaries are ignored, love is not present.

Closing Truth

This Man Trap caused the greatest harm to my body and my sense of self. For months, I blamed myself and internalised shame, blame, and guilt. I had to do deep inner child healing and truly believe that this was not my fault. That's how blurred the lines were. Consent is NOT a grey area. A NO means a NO. This test is not about blaming yourself.

The fact here is that we are dealing with a type of man who has zero respect for boundaries. He is a predator because he somehow feels entitled to any woman who crosses his path. Such is the level of his darkness, and this is exactly what rapists are made of.

The unflinching truth is that a man must be so in tune with the concept of consent that even the slightest discomfort from a woman is a signal enough. Even if you take away one thing from this book, may it be the power of consent. And consent is about returning authority to the body.

Let's talk about the real C-word.

Consent.

It is astonishing — tragic, really — that in 2026 we still need to define it. That grown men still confuse arousal with entitlement. That a biological reflex is treated like a contractual obligation signed by a woman's body. So many times, I have heard this phrase "I am erect now, what about me." My consent be damned!

An erection is not a binding agreement.

It is not a down payment.

It is not a green signal that overrides a woman's nervous system, intuition, or shifting desire.

Consent is not a one-time clearance stamp. It is a living, breathing agreement between two sovereign beings. And the moment one sovereign being says "no" — whether softly, angrily, awkwardly, or after previously saying "yes" — everything stops.

Not pauses.

Not negotiates.

Stops.

What unsettles me most is how quickly some men collapse into injury when denied access. As if a woman withdrawing consent, is a personal attack. As if her boundary is cruelty. As if his temporary discomfort outweighs her permanent memory of violation.

This is where the trap lies.

We have socialized women to manage male arousal like it is a fragile emergency. To soothe it. To accommodate it. To prioritize it. To avoid "making a scene." To endure discomfort so that he doesn't feel rejected.

And that is how dehumanization disguises itself as romance.

A woman is not a pacifier for male desire.

She is not a warm solution to a physiological inconvenience.

She is not a prop in the story of his hunger.

She is a person. With a body that can change its mind. With a nervous system that can shift from safety to alarm in seconds. With intuition that may register something before language does.

Consent is not just about permission. It is about presence. Mutuality. It is about two people wanting the same thing at the same time — not one convincing, coaxing, guilting, or emotionally cornering the other into compliance.

If your arousal requires her silence, her hesitation, or her dissociation, it is not passion. It is entitlement.

And entitlement is not sexy. It is predatory.

The most powerful man in the room is not the one who pushes through resistance. It is the one who can hold his desire without weaponizing it. The one who can hear "no" without shrinking, shaming, or retaliating. The one who understands that self-regulation is masculinity.

If consent changes, the answer changes.

If she freezes, the answer is no.

If she withdraws, the answer is no.

If she hesitates, the answer is no.

There is nothing confusing about this.

The real tragedy is not that women say no.

The tragedy is that so many men were never taught that no is sacred

Liberation begins when women learn to trust sensation before story and to exit where consent and boundaries are not honoured.

CHAPTER 5

THE NARCISSIST MAN TRAP

The Narcissist Man Trap is the one most empaths stumble into at least once in their lifetime- because it doesn't look like danger at first. It looks like intensity. It looks like chemistry. It looks like attention, devotion, and a kind of admiration that feels like a warm spotlight after years of surviving in the dark.

And so did I.

It was my father-wound that made me vulnerable to this particular trap- the hunger to finally be seen, to finally be chosen, to finally be held by a masculine presence who didn't collapse into rage or silence. So, when F entered my life, I didn't see a narcissist. I saw the possibility.

He love-bombed and charmed me with expertise.

Cooking for me, taking me out on curated dates, staying up late talking for hours, holding my face like I was the centre of his universe. The emotional intensity was intoxicating. The physical chemistry was volcanic. And in my unhealed state, I made the most common, fatal mistake:

I mistook chemistry for connection.

I mistook intensity for intimacy.

I mistook familiarity for fate.

The first red flag announced itself quietly, like a whisper I ignored. He spoke about his past relationships- every single one of them- with contempt and blame. According to him, all his exes were "crazy," "ungrateful," "selfish," "immature," "toxic." And get this- he referred to them as narcissists- Ha! The irony!

Not once did he mention his own role in any of those breakages.

Even in my abusive marriage, I had still reflected on my own patterns. But F? Oh, he could do no wrong. He was God's gift to woman-kind, you, see?

F was the hero of every story.

F was the victim of every woman.

That should've been my cue to run, but the father wound in me lingered, listening, hoping, bargaining with God.

And then began the emotional roller coaster.

Three months.

Three breakups. I didn't know what on again, off again meant until this one came along.

Three cycles of idealisation, devaluation, and discard.

A pattern so textbook it could have been printed in a clinical manual.

He nitpicked over the smallest things- my food habits, my schedule, my boundaries, even the frequency with which I used the restroom. Nothing was too trivial for his criticism. And beneath this surface-level irritation lay something even darker: a deep obsession with control.

Slowly, almost imperceptibly, the love bombing turned into microaggressions.

Microaggressions turned into criticism.

Criticism turned into gaslighting.

When I confronted him about the emotional volatility, he didn't reflect or take responsibility. He twisted the narrative. In true narcissistic fashion, he flipped the script so fast my mind struggled to keep up. I'd walk into conversations feeling hurt and walk out apologising for things I never did.

And then came the foul language.

The moment his veneer cracked.

That was when something in me- something ancient, something hard-earned- finally snapped.

I stepped off the carousel.

I stepped out of the trance.

I stepped away from the pattern I had inherited from my father.

Leaving him wasn't just a breakup.

It was an exorcism.

A severing.

A liberation.

It was the moment I realised I wasn't looking for love anymore- I was reclaiming myself.

After I stepped away, something in my heart expanded. The heaviness lifted. The fog dissolved. My soul felt lighter, brighter, more spacious. For the first time in years, I could hear my own voice again. And with that clarity came the most important understanding of my journey so far:

I am the happiest when I fly solo.

My peace was never meant to be shared with chaos.

My heart was never meant to host someone else's wounds.

The Narcissist Man Trap taught me something no relationship ever had:

that freedom, sovereignty, and self-love feel better than any temporary high of being adored by the wrong man.

It taught me that breaking a relationship is sometimes the only way to heal a lifelong wound.

And when I broke this one, I finally broke the father-wound too.

This chapter of my life was not about losing him. It was my first real step in finding myself. This one truly marked the opening of my heart centre. Why? Because I finally shifted this paradigm of looking for approval, of looking for love and validation from someone who replicated my father energetically and emotionally.

The Shadow Patterns of a Narcissist

- Classic Love-Bombing, which quickly turns to criticism as the relationship progresses
- When you object, gaslighting and victimising themselves, twisting the narrative
- Possessive nature, beware of phrases "You are mine and mine alone." "You belong to me forever." Yes, their forever lasts a few weeks as soon as you stop adhering to their playbook. They don't care about sustaining the relationship. They are hooked on the chase.

What makes the Narcissist Man Trap so dangerous is not cruelty at the start—it is intensity. The body mistakes intensity for aliveness, attention for safety, and admiration for love. This trap does not begin with harm. It begins with activation.

Which is why the body must be trained to read patterns, not promises.

The Narcissistic Man Trap: Why Empathy Is the Bait

If there were an Olympic sport for emotional seduction, the Narcissistic Man would already have a gold medal, a sob story, and an ex he swears was "crazy."

This trap is one of the most effective in the modern dating ecosystem—not because women are foolish, naïve, or desperate, but because many women are wired for empathy. We are listeners.

We are attuned. We feel other people's pain as if it were our own. And the narcissist, like a highly trained emotional predator, can smell this from across the room.

He doesn't read your résumé.

He reads your nervous system.

The moment he senses that you are warm, compassionate, perceptive—that you soften when someone shares pain—he knows exactly which script to pull out. And he has rehearsed this one extensively.

Enter: The Sob Story.

It arrives early. Too early. Often, within the first few dates, sometimes within the first hour. He tells you about his difficult childhood, his emotionally unavailable parent, his heartbreak, his betrayal. He speaks with just enough vulnerability to feel intimate, but not enough accountability to be real.

And there it is—that look in your eyes.

The "oh my poor baby" look.

The micro-tilt of the head.

The softening of the chest.

The instinct to hold, soothe, and understand.

And Bam! You have entered the trap.

From that moment on, the dynamic quietly shifts. You are no longer an equal. You are a resource.

The Narcissistic Man is not interested in mutual intimacy; he is interested in emotional supply. Your empathy becomes his fuel. Your curiosity becomes his stage. Your compassion becomes his camouflage.

He moves with extraordinary stealth. There is no sudden cruelty, no obvious red flags. Instead, there is intensity—fast bonding, deep conversations, grand gestures, magnetic charm. He mirrors your values, praises your depth, and tells you how "different" you are from everyone else.

Which is exactly what he told the last one.

And the one before that.

The narcissist's charm is not accidental. It is cultivated through sheer practice. He has studied reactions, tested scripts, and refined his timing. He knows when to withdraw just enough to make you lean in, when to compliment, when to sulk, and when to play wounded.

Meanwhile, your empathy—your greatest strength—is being quietly weaponised against you.

You begin explaining his behaviour.

You begin giving him the benefit of the doubt.

You begin holding space while he holds none.

And slowly, almost imperceptibly, the relationship centres around his emotions, his needs, his grievances.

A crucial telltale sign emerges early, if you know how to spot it: everyone in his past is the villain.

The ex was abusive.

The mother was controlling.

The boss was threatened by him.

The friends betrayed him.

He is always both the hero and the victim. A tragic protagonist in an endless series of misunderstandings caused by other people's inadequacies.

This is not bad luck.

This is a pattern.

Another red flag disguised as intimacy is trauma dumping. When someone unloads deeply personal pain far too soon, it can feel like trust—but it is often a boundary violation. True intimacy unfolds gradually. Narcissistic intimacy is fast, overwhelming, and one-sided.

It is designed to bypass your discernment.

And here's the uncomfortable truth: many women are conditioned to mistake emotional intensity for depth. We are taught that if someone shares pain, they must be genuine. That if someone is wounded, they deserve patience. That love means staying, understanding, fixing.

But empathy without discernment is not love—it is exposure.

Your empathy is not the problem.

Your lack of boundaries around it is.

The Narcissistic Man does not fall in love with you. He falls in love with how you make him feel—seen, soothed, validated, admired. And the moment you stop providing that without question—when you ask for reciprocity, consistency, or accountability—the charm begins to flicker.

Suddenly, you are "too sensitive."

Too demanding.

Too much.

The same empathy that once made you special is now used as evidence against you.

This is why this trap is so effective. It doesn't ensnare through force. It seduces through resonance. It uses your goodness as bait and your hope as glue.

The Narcissistic Man is the Venus flytrap of the dating world—beautiful, intriguing, seemingly open. You lean in gently, drawn by the promise of connection, and by the time you realise what's happening, the door has quietly closed behind you.

The lesson here is not to harden. It is to be refined. Discernment is the key.

Discernment is empathy with a backbone.

It is the ability to notice when vulnerability lacks accountability. When stories replace self-reflection. When intimacy feels rushed rather than earned. When you are being pulled into a caretaker role before you have even chosen the person.

You are not here to heal men who refuse to heal themselves.

You are not cruel for pausing.

You are not cold for observing.

You are not unloving for walking away.

Empathy, when grounded in self-respect, becomes wisdom.

And the moment you stop mistaking emotional performance for emotional maturity, the Narcissistic Man loses his power—not because you changed who you are, but because you finally chose yourself.

Venus flytraps only work on creatures that don't realise they're being fed on.

Now you know.

A 10-Step Somatic Test for Detecting the Narcissist Man Trap

This test is not about diagnosing a man.

It is about listening to what your nervous system already knows.

You do not need all ten.

Three is enough to pause. Five is enough to leave.

1. **The Nervous System Hijack Test**
   Notice: Do you feel unusually activated around him?
   This can look like:

- Racing thoughts
- Sleeplessness after interactions
- A constant "buzz" in the chest
- A sense of urgency or obsession

Red flag: When your body is stimulated but not soothed.

Healthy connection regulates.

Narcissistic intensity dysregulates. It is addictive at first. What rises with this intensity will also come crashing down with the same intensity. It's plain physics.

2. **The Spotlight Sensation Test**

   Ask: Do I feel "chosen" rather than seen?

   Early on, narcissistic attention feels like:

   - Being admired rather than understood
   - Being idealised rather than known
   - Being placed on a pedestal instead of being met on the ground

   Red flag: If you feel elevated but not emotionally held.

   Pedestals are unstable structures.

3. **The Body Shrink Test**

   After spending time with him, does your body:

   - Feel smaller?
   - Feel tighter?
   - Feel like it's monitoring itself?

   Red flag: When your body starts performing instead of relaxing.

   Love expands the body.

   Control contracts it. Subtle control will start arriving even at the early stages.

4. **The Self-Abandonment Test**

   Do you notice yourself:

   - Over-explaining
   - Editing your needs
   - Softening your boundaries to keep the peace

   Red flag: If your body starts negotiating against itself. Any relationship that requires self-erasure is unsafe.

5. **The Emotional Whiplash Test**

   Do interactions leave you:

   - Elated one day
   - Anxious the next
   - Confused about where you stand

   Red flag: Inconsistency is not complexity—it is destabilization. Dating a narcissist is an emotional rollercoaster. They have unresolved anger and pain, do not believe in therapy and hence project all that wounding on you.

6. **The Gut Silence Test**

   Do you stop checking in with your intuition because:

   - He seems "so sure"
   - He reframes your doubts as insecurity
   - He positions himself as more evolved or knowledgeable

   Red flag: When your inner voice goes quiet, not calm. They say they are even beyond therapy because "they know better." This is a huge red flag

7. **The Tension-in-the-Yes Test**

   When you agree to something with him, does your body:

   - Tighten?
   - Hesitate?

- Feel a subtle resistance?

Red flag: A "yes" that carries tension is not consent—it is compliance.

8. **The Ex-Story Pattern Test**

   When he talks about past relationships, notice your body.

   If you feel:

   - Uneasy
   - Defensive on behalf of women you've never met
   - A tightening when he blames everyone but himself

   Red flag: A man without self-reflection will eventually make you the villain. In all his past relationships, somehow, he was the saint and all his exes were the villains.

9. **The Emotional Aftertaste Test**

   After conflict or "resolution," do you feel:

   - Drained rather than settled
   - Guilty rather than clear
   - Responsible for his emotions

   Red flag: Narcissists are master-minds at this game. They create the problem- you react- then they play the victim. This is their classic game and you can't win. Exit is the only strategy here. Repair that costs you your peace is not repair.

10. **The Simplicity Test (Final Gate)**

    Ask your body, quietly:

    "Do I feel safe being fully myself here?"

    If the answer is anything other than a grounded yes—

    pause.

    The body never lies.

    It only gets ignored.

Detecting Love-Bombing Early (Before You Get Hooked)

Love-bombing is not love.

It is emotional acceleration without containment.

Here is how to spot it early—before attachment takes root.

1. **Speed Without Substance**
   He escalates:
   - Emotional intimacy
   - Physical closeness
   - Future talk- starts calling you his wife in month two of dating, or "his forever."

   Before:
   - Trust
   - Consistency
   - Time

   Truth: Real intimacy unfolds. It does not rush.
2. **Excessive Focus Without Curiosity**
   He is:
   - Intensely attentive

   But not deeply curious about your inner world
   Truth: Attention is not attunement.
3. **Grand Gestures, Shallow Repair**
   He dazzles with:
   - Dates
   - Words
   - Plans

   But struggles with:

- Accountability
- Repair
- Listening when challenged

Truth: Love is revealed in conflict, not charm.

4. **Idealisation Language**

   Phrases like:

   - "You're not like other women"
   - "I've never felt this before"
   - "You're perfect for me"

   Truth: No one who truly sees you believes you are perfect.

5. **Your Body Feels Addicted, Not Anchored**

   You crave:

   - The high
   - The attention
   - The reassurance

   Truth: Love feels steady. Addiction feels urgent.

When the Veneer Cracks

How Narcissists Begin Finding Fault in Everything

The shift is rarely sudden.

It is incremental, strategic, and deeply disorienting.

1. **From Praise to Policing**

   What he once adored becomes:

   - Critiqued
   - Corrected
   - Controlled

   Your habits, tone, timing, and preferences all come under scrutiny.

2. **Micro-Criticisms Disguised as "Concern"**
   "You could do better if…"
   "I'm just being honest…"
   "I'm trying to help you grow…"
   Growth that shames is not growth.
3. **Gaslighting Through Emotional Reversal**
   You enter conversations hurt.
   You leave apologising.
   When reality keeps flipping, trust the pattern—not the explanation.
4. **Fault-Finding During Vulnerability**
   Your moments of openness become:
   - Weaponized
   - Mocked
   - Revisited during arguments

   Emotional safety is gone when vulnerability becomes ammunition.
5. **Withholding as Punishment**
   Affection, warmth, or communication is withdrawn when you assert yourself.
   Love that disappears when challenged was never stable. And you are called "too sensitive, unreasonable, overactive."
6. **Escalation of Contempt**
   Sarcasm.
   Dismissiveness.
   Foul language.
   Contempt is the point of no return.
7. **You Begin Monitoring Yourself**
   You:

- Watch your words
- Pre-empt reactions
- Shrink to avoid conflict

This is not love.

This is survival mode.

Closing Truth of This Chapter

The Narcissist Man Trap does not teach you about him.

It teaches you about where you learned to confuse intensity with love.

Leaving is not failure.

It is completion.

Sometimes the relationship must break so the wound can finally close.

When you walk away from the narcissist, you are not losing love.

You are reclaiming:

- Your nervous system
- Your self-trust
- Your sovereignty-in-formation

And the greatest truth of all:

Peace is not boring.

Chaos was simply familiar.

This chapter is not about heartbreak.

It is about liberation.

And liberation always begins the moment you stop asking to be chosen and start choosing yourself.

CHAPTER 6

THE TRAUMA BOND MAN TRAP

This was the potential. The one I loved the hardest and the one I fought for the hardest. It was also the most difficult labyrinth to decipher- and truth be told, after so many years, I still haven't quite figured this one out fully.

The man who taught me the most and broke me the deepest.

Let's call him Z.

If my life were a series of karmic exams, Z was the greatest one- the test, the one that decides whether you ascend or collapse.

I have loved many men, but Z…

Z was the one my soul recognised before my mind could warn me.

The one who mirrored my deepest wounds and my highest potential so flawlessly that for a long time, I mistook pain for destiny.

THE DANCE OF MIRRORS

From the beginning, our boundaries were so permeable that it was impossible to tell where he ended and where I began. We would trigger each other into 6-hour-long arguments that circled the same wound again and again until we were both breathless, blue in the face, unable to tell who started it or what we were even fighting for.

It was like two mirrors reflecting fractures back and forth.

We weren't solving anything. We were combusting.

Our wounding was magnified. Our longing was magnetised.

And our attempts to repair were like infants trying to perform open-heart surgery on each other.

Because here's the truth:

I was the classic anxious attachment.

He was the textbook avoidant.

Together, we were a psychological tsunami.

THE SWING

He would swing between extremes so fast it made my nervous system crackle like a live wire.

One moment, he was the kindest man I had ever known-thoughtful, attuned, gentle, full of gestures that melted years of defensive armour.

The next moment, he was harsh, cold, reactive- words cut like knives, blame like bullets, silence like abandonment.

This cycle continued not just when we dated, but well into our friendship. A friendship built on trauma residues and dopamine highs.

Cortisol.

Dopamine.

Cortisol.

Dopamine.

My body knew the rhythm before my mind caught up.

And the part that really drew me in was:

He was there for me in my darkest times. The times when most people stepped away, terrified of my anguish, but Z stayed. That created a soul-deep loyalty from my end. The times I was suicidal, the times when I was breaking down, spiralling. He soothed and stroked me- my nervous system would unwind- for that brief breath of fresh air. The kind of air that one is gasping for and fighting to stay alive for.

And my wounded inner child mistook this for unconditional love.

THE MYTH I FELL FOR

I had a theory, a naïve one:

"If someone is there for you at your worst, they'll be there for you… always."

So, I pursued him relentlessly for two years.

I chased, I yearned, I convinced myself he was "the one."

But here's the brutal truth:

In pursuing him, I abandoned myself.

Over and over and over again.

Every time, I tolerated the ambiguity.

Every time, I excused the harshness.

Every time I settled for half-love, half-attention, half-presence.

THE KARMIC ENTANGLEMENT

We weren't lovers.

We were two wounded teenagers trapped in adult bodies, reenacting our primal trauma that was never healed.

My inner teen was:

1. Abandoned
2. Anxious
3. Codependent
4. Desperate for rescue

His inner teen was:

1. Avoidant

2. Controlling
3. Triggered by intimacy
4. Harsh when emotionally overwhelmed

Together, we were a karmic fiasco. Our bond was so intense that it felt orchestrated by something higher- some divine intelligence that knows exactly which buttons to push, to force you into self-love and sovereignty. And this is where I grasped the unicorn I like to mention- self-love.

There were moments his hugs calmed every chaotic molecule in my body. There were moments his words sent me spiralling so violently I couldn't breathe. He would soothe my nervous system…and shock it again almost instantly.

It was spiritual.

It was psychological.

It was chemical.

It was karmic.

THE INNER CHILD WAR

We threw tantrums at each other like two feral teenagers trapped in a burning house.

Neither backing down. Neither self-regulating. Neither knowing how to pause.

We fought until both of us spiralled into emotional madness- hours, sometimes days of chaos.

People say trauma bonds are addictive.

But they don't tell you the real truth:

Trauma bonds feel like union at first.

They feel like destiny. They feel like home.

But here's the truth- trauma doesn't feel like home because it's love.

It feels like home because it's familiar.

The Hook- The Addictive Spiral

The pattern was almost always the same-

- the relief after chaos
- the apology after the rage
- the tenderness after the storm
- the soft voice after the harsh words

He became both the poison and the antidote. That is the signature of a trauma bond.

THE FINAL REALIZATION

If I trace the lines backwards, here's what I see:

This was a learning ground- love- the one that prepares you the most. I fell for his potential, not where he really was. My greatest folly was that I was looking to be rescued. He didn't rescue me. He pushed me to rescue myself.

He was not my soulmate.

He was my mirror.

My karmic exam.

My emotional detox.

My dark night catalyst.

The trauma bond was not a trap meant to destroy me- It was the furnace meant to forge me.

I walked through it addicted, blind, hopeful, lost- and I walked out sovereign.

While navigating trauma bonds, I realised something- there is no formula for how long it will take for you to "get over" someone. The person remains in our system like a karmic imprint until the lesson is learnt. That could be hours or years, until we learn what we are meant to; the dynamic can become a loop in our nervous system. Be gentle with yourself, while remaining strong in your sovereignty as you navigate this.

WHAT IS A TRAUMA BOND (Beyond the Buzzword)

A trauma bond is not simply an unhealthy attachment. It is a neuro-emotional addiction formed through cycles of intensity, rupture, and intermittent repair. It develops when emotional pain and emotional relief are delivered by the same person, wiring the nervous system to associate love with dysregulation.

At its core, a trauma bond is a survival bond, not a love bond.

It is forged when:

- Connection is inconsistent
- Affection is unpredictable

- Safety is periodically withdrawn and restored

This inconsistency creates a powerful loop in the nervous system. The body learns that closeness is followed by threat, and threat is followed by closeness. Over time, the system stops seeking peace and starts seeking relief.

Trauma bonds often feel spiritual, karmic, or fated, not because they are divine unions, but because they activate early attachment wounds stored below conscious memory. The intensity feels transcendent because it bypasses logic and goes straight to the limbic system.

Love in a trauma bond is not chosen.

It is activated.

WHY WOMEN FALL FOR TRAUMA BONDS

(And How They Mirror the Father Wound, Mother Wound—or Both)

Women do not fall into trauma bonds because they are weak. They fall into them because they are wired for connection and often conditioned to tolerate emotional inconsistency.

1. The Father Wound Mirror

When the father was:

- Emotionally unavailable
- Inconsistent
- Affectionate but withdrawn
- Loving yet unpredictable

The nervous system learns:

"Love must be earned. Attention is intermittent. Presence is not guaranteed."

A man who oscillates between closeness and distance feels familiar, not dangerous. The woman keeps trying—not because she lacks self-respect, but because her body remembers this rhythm as love.

2. The Mother Wound Mirror

When the mother was:

- Emotionally overwhelmed
- Anxious or enmeshed projects her fears, calling it love and concern
- In need of emotional caretaking

The child learns:

"I must manage emotions to stay connected."

In adulthood, this shows up as:

- Over-functioning
- Emotional vigilance
- Confusing caretaking with intimacy
- Peace-keeping
- Managing their own anger and hurt, which usually looks like suppressing them

The woman feels needed, important, indispensable—until she is depleted.

3. When Both Wounds Are Present

This is where trauma bonds become most addictive.

The woman:

- Chases emotional availability (father wound)
- Over-gives and self-abandons (mother wound)

The man:

- Withdraws under intimacy and commitment
- Returns with intensity

Together, they recreate the original attachment ecosystem. The bond feels ancient, inevitable, cosmic—because it is anchored in early survival wiring.

This is not romance.

This is repetition seeking resolution.

THE SOMATIC CHECKLIST

How the Nervous System Identifies a Trauma Bond

(During conflict and after conflict)

A trauma bond is best identified in the body, not the story. Use this checklist to assess with precision.

During Conflict

- Heart rate spikes rapidly, often out of proportion to the actual issue- the conflict is blown out of proportion by either or both sides
- Tightening of the chest or throat, as if words are stuck or unsafe

- Tunnel vision—inability to see nuance or alternatives- or resolve the conflict calmly
- Compulsion to explain, prove, or be understood at all costs
- Loss of time awareness (arguments lasting hours without resolution)

After Conflict

- Sudden relief or collapse once contact is restored
- Exhaustion bordering on emotional shutdown
- Confusion—forgetting why the conflict felt so intense
- Strong craving for reassurance, touch, or closeness- this is where the nervous system craves soothing, and this is exactly where the addiction intensifies
- Temporary calm followed by delayed anxiety or dread

Overall Nervous System Pattern

- The body feels activated rather than settled after "repair"
- Peace feels unfamiliar; intensity feels intimate- the highs are very high and lows are debilitating
- Silence feels threatening, not neutral
- Relief is mistaken for love
- Calm feels boring or unsafe

Key Marker:

If connection soothes you only after dysregulation, you are not bonding—you are regulating through another person.

Closing Integration

A healthy bond expands the nervous system.

A trauma bond contracts it—then briefly relieves it.

One builds capacity.

The other builds dependency. What feels like destiny is often just the body asking to finally be healed. The trauma-bond is the masterpiece of your childhood wounds.

CHAPTER 7

THE PSEUDO-SPIRITUALIST MAN TRAP

Ah, yes- the Pseudo-Spiritualist Man Trap.

The one that smells like sandalwood, speaks like a sage, and behaves like a sales pitch.

Let's call him V.

V was the prototype of a certain species of man floating around in spiritual spaces today: the Enlightened Bro.

Typically found wearing a white linen dhoti or harem pants, carrying a mala, and having just returned from the Osho Ashram with a freshly manufactured aura of "inner peace."

He had done a couple of meditation retreats, learned a few buzzwords, and suddenly believed he was the reincarnation of Bodhidharma with an Instagram handle.

But the truth?

The man was simply attracted to my looks and my pin code.

Under the façade of "deep spiritual connection," he was actually fantasising about shifting into the posh part of Mumbai where I lived. Because, of course, enlightenment flows better when the WiFi is fast, and the building has valet parking.

V used to work as a copywriter- which, in hindsight, explained everything. He knew how to market anything, including himself. Within weeks of meeting me, he was claiming he knew over 150 meditation techniques. One hundred and fifty!

Even the Buddha would be impressed.

And then he did the inevitable: he began facilitating Osho's Dynamic Meditation- that extremely powerful, cathartic, potentially overwhelming practice with zero training, grounding, or therapeutic understanding. If a participant had a trauma response during one of his "facilitations," his response would probably be to chant louder about the theatrics of "deep peace."

The reality of V was- he was simply a charismatic man who figured out that spirituality is profitable, that enlightenment is a brand, and that Instagram loves a man who lights incense on Reels.

I realised quickly that V was not a spiritual practitioner- he was a spiritual PowerPoint presentation.

All packaging.

No presence.

All talk.

No embodiment.

He even claimed he had "taken sanyasa," which is such blasphemy when you consider he was simultaneously trying to transcend vulnerable women into "higher states" of enlightenment-preferably in his bedroom.

This is the part that infuriates me:

The dark side of spirituality today is not demons-it is hypocrisy disguised as mastery.

It's people who read one book, attend one retreat, or survive one heartbreak and suddenly declare themselves gurus. In today's world, the barrier to becoming a healer is tragically low. Two days of a workshop, a certificate with a lotus on it, and bam, you're a "trauma-informed facilitator."

Trauma? What trauma?

Knowledge, Wisdom? From where?

Here is the raw truth:

A healer is not made in a weekend intensive.

A healer is forged in the underworld.

A healer is someone who has walked through their own darkness, not someone who purchased a mala and memorised the word 'Namaste.'

A real healer carries light because they have wrestled with their own shadows.

A real healer is a conduit of the divine- not a prisoner of greed.

A real healer knows how to hold a soul without exploiting a body. And V- well, V was a phoney.

So, did I stay?

Absolutely not.

I walked away with the quiet efficiency of a woman who has learned to trust her intuition louder than anyone's chanting. This one didn't even deserve a dramatic exit. I simply saw the fraudulence and stepped out of the frame.

But this experience left me with a valuable mirror- a mirror reflecting the spiritual bypassing epidemic of our time. People want shortcuts to awakening. They want the crown without the cave. The halo without the heart work. The guru role without the soul.

The Pseudo-Spiritualist Man Trap is exactly that:

a man who performs spirituality instead of living it.

A man who talks about peace because he cannot practice honesty.

A man who knows meditations by number but not by depth.

And the lesson here is simple:

Spirituality without embodiment is just performance.

Healing without humility is manipulation.

And no amount of Osho quotes can hide an unhealed masculine.

Sometimes, the most spiritual thing you can do is walk away from the people pretending to be spiritual.

And that, my loves, is exactly what I did.

Case 2- The Ponytail Prophet

This one arrived in a man bun, and an inflated sense of cosmic entitlement- wrapped in a ponytail and a reputation.

A "well-known" astrologer.

A self-appointed interpreter of destiny.

A man who believed the stars existed primarily to explain why women should want him.

I met him almost six years ago, at a time when I still believed love was something one had to chase after—as though partnership was a rare species that required spiritual pilgrimage, emotional endurance, and the willingness to ignore one's own discomfort in the name of growth.

He found me on Facebook.

Slid into my DMs with the confidence of a man who had never been questioned.

Called me a shamanic tantrika.

Now, in hindsight, this phrase reads like a red flag stitched in gold thread. But at the time? It landed. Of course it did. Nothing activates a spiritually hungry woman faster than a stranger who claims to see her essence in twelve words or fewer.

I was headed to Goa anyway—for a healer conference, no less. The universe, it seemed, was conspiring. Or so I thought. (Note:

how the mind creates incredible webs of spiritual lingo- like destiny, karmic union etc., to make you believe- this could be it).

We met. There was chemistry, in the way there is chemistry when two people mistake intensity for meaning. He read my chart. Without being asked. And then—this is where the comedy truly begins—he solemnly informed me that we were incompatible in partnership.

Excuse me.

Did I apply?

Was there a form I missed?

It was day two, and already this man had appointed himself gatekeeper of my romantic destiny. The assumption was so casual, so unconscious, that it barely registered as arrogance. It was simply normal to him that any woman in proximity must be evaluated for mating potential.

Within days, his controlling tendencies surfaced. Comments about my lifestyle. Subtle corrections. Gentle superiority masked as guidance. Before I could reject him, he had pre-emptively rejected me—citing the stars, of course. Nothing bruises the ego quite like cosmic outsourcing.

And then… silence.

Years passed.

I grew.

He aged.

The ponytail, apparently, endured.

Out of nowhere, he resurfaced. A message infused with faux depth and spiritual intimacy. He claimed that only he could understand me. That my "energetic complexities" were too rare for ordinary men. That the world was lonely for people like us.

Translation: he was lonely. And horny. And hoping astrology could do what authenticity could not.

By this point, I had evolved enough to ask questions rather than absorb narratives. I asked him why he was reaching out now, after being so certain we were "misaligned." I asked what had changed—him, me, or the stars.

His answers were evasive. Circular. Mystical in the way con artists are mystical when cornered.

And then came the slideshow.

Yes.

A slideshow.

A carefully curated montage of my photos—assembled without consent and sent with the expectation of gratitude. It was meant to be flattering. It was not. It was intimate in the way surveillance is intimate.

He video-called me shortly after. And there it was—that look. The one thing women across cultures and centuries have learned to identify in under three seconds. The look that says: I am not here for your soul.

I declined. Clearly.

Silence again.

Until one evening, after some conversational back-and-forth, he made his real request. He asked me to show him my body type on video.

No metaphor.

No poetry.

No tantra.

Just entitlement.

And when I hesitated—when my sovereign adult stepped in—he revealed the truth with accidental brilliance.

"It took you three hours to get here," he said. "That was enough for me to know."

Enough to know what, exactly?

That his grand narrative of cosmic partnership was nothing more than a poorly disguised attempt at a sex video call.

I hung up.

No dramatic monologue.

No spiritual debate.

Just a clean exit.

This is the pseudo-spiritualist man trap in its purest form: a man who uses sacred language to bypass consent, destiny to override discernment, and mysticism to justify entitlement.

He does not seek union.

He seeks access.

He does not honour the feminine.

He consumes it.

And the real lesson here was not about him.

It was about me.

The woman who once chased meaning across continents had become someone who no longer negotiated her boundaries in the name of connection. The stars no longer impressed me. Presence did.

The ponytail prophet faded back into the algorithm, where men like him belong—mistaken for wisdom, powered by ego, and entirely undone by a woman who knows how to hang up.

Let's take this up a notch, shall we? Unfortunately, the spiritual and healing communities are infiltrated by these predators masquerading as gurus.

Pseudo-spiritualism has now reached its peak mutation, especially in the neo-tantra circus. Tantra- which is meant to be a sacred unison of energy with the divine, a deep merging of consciousness and presence- is being bastardised into chaotic workshops where it becomes a sexual free-for-all disguised as enlightenment.

What once required lifetimes of discipline, devotion, and inner purification is now reduced to festival tents filled with psychedelics, breathwork theatrics, and thousands of vulnerable participants- mostly women- being encouraged to "liberate themselves" by gyrating on strangers who then take undue advantage of them. This is not Tantra. This is a chemically induced high from sex and drugs that you could get at a rave or a rock concert. Real Tantra awakens the divine; fake Tantra awakens the libido. And what we see today is not a sacred union, but a spiritualized buffet of bodies where sexual energy is exploited, not honoured- and the divine is the first thing to disappear from the room.

The Dangerous Shadow of the Pseudo-Spiritualist Man Trap

This trap is not merely disappointing.

It is dangerous.

Because unlike other man traps that operate in bars, apps, or bedrooms, the Pseudo-Spiritualist Man often operates in healing, therapeutic, and spiritual spaces—places where vulnerability is not incidental but intentional. These men do not stumble upon intimacy; they position themselves inside it.

They call themselves facilitators, healers, guides, tantriks, astrologers, coaches, shamans. They borrow the language of the divine while serving something far more debase: power, sex, and money.

What makes this trap particularly insidious is that it hides behind trust. In spaces designed for opening, surrender, and emotional safety, discernment is often framed as "ego," boundaries as "fear," and scepticism as "lack of faith." The predator thrives precisely where questioning is discouraged.

The pseudo-spiritual predator is not working for the divine.

He is working the room.

Below are seven shadow patterns that define this trap:

1. **Spiritual Authority Without Accountability**
   He claims access to higher truth but resists oversight, supervision, or peer accountability. Anyone who questions him is "unconscious," "triggered," or "not ready for the work."
2. **Manufactured Intimacy**
   He accelerates closeness through rituals, eye-gazing, energy work, or trauma disclosure—creating a false sense of soul-bonding without earned trust.
3. **Eroticisation of Healing**
   Touch, sexuality, or tantric language are introduced prematurely, framed as "medicine" rather than desire. Consent becomes blurred under spiritual justification.
4. **Bypassing Boundaries as Enlightenment**
   Your discomfort is reframed as resistance. Your hesitation becomes a blockage. Your no is interpreted as fear rather than sovereignty.
5. **Trauma Harvesting**
   He encourages repeated storytelling of pain—not to integrate it, but to bind you to him emotionally. Your wounds become his leverage.

6. **Guru Inflation**

   He positions himself as rare, chosen, misunderstood—someone who alone can "hold" you. This isolates you from other supports and inflates dependency.
7. **Transactional Enlightenment**

   Healing is dangled like a carrot—accessible only through continued access to him, his sessions, his body, his approval.

This is not spirituality.

It is predation wrapped in his harem pants.

Why Women Seeking Healing Are Especially Vulnerable to This Trap

Women do not enter healing spaces frivolously. They arrive carrying grief, exhaustion, heartbreak, trauma, and longing—for relief, meaning, and safety. Many are already depleted by caregiving, emotional labour, and years of prioritising others over themselves. When a man presents himself as someone who "understands," who speaks gently, who names pain accurately, it can feel like rescue.

Healing seekers are often:

- Actively unarmouring
- Practising openness
- Learning to trust
- Letting go of hypervigilance

These are not weaknesses.

They are states of receptivity.

And receptivity, when met by the wrong person, becomes exposure.

This vulnerability is not limited to spiritual circles. It extends to therapy rooms, coaching containers, yoga studios, breathwork circles, retreats, and even informal "support" spaces. Anywhere pain is present, and authority is assumed, the risk exists.

What deepens the injustice is that when harm occurs in these spaces, women are often blamed twice: first by the perpetrator, then by the culture. "Why didn't you see it?" "Why did you trust him?" "Did you misinterpret his intention?"

But healing spaces are meant to be safe by design. When men exploit them, it is not a personal failure of discernment—it is a systemic breach of ethics.

These encounters do more than disappoint. They re-traumatise. They teach women that even in spaces meant for repair, their bodies are still consumable, their pain still profitable, their trust still extractable.

The deepest wound is not sexual or emotional—it is existential. The feeling that nowhere is safe to soften.

This is why naming this trap matters.

Because women deserve healing without being hunted.

Somatic Checklist: Identifying the Pseudo-Spiritualist Man Trap

(In romantic, therapeutic, or healing contexts)

Use the body—not the story.

1. Your body feels porous, not supported after interactions—like your edges have dissolved without grounding.
2. You feel subtly indebted—as though insight, attention, or healing must be repaid with availability.
3. Your breath shortens when boundaries arise, even if the words sound "loving."
4. You feel special but unstable—elevated one moment, anxious the next.
5. Your intuition tightens while your mind rationalises ("He's just advanced.")
6. There is pressure to stay open, even when something inside wants to slow down.
7. Your body contracts around touch, but your mind overrides it as "healing."
8. You leave sessions confused, emotionally stirred, but not integrated.
9. You feel seen but not held—noticed, named, but not contained.
10. Your nervous system feels dysregulated, not resourced, after repeated contact.

Healing should create coherence, not dependency.

Safety should deepen agency, not blur it.

The Pseudo-Spiritualist Man Trap thrives where women are taught to surrender faster than they are taught to protect themselves.

But spirituality without embodiment is performance.

Healing without ethics is exploitation.

And sometimes, the most sacred act is not opening your heart—but walking away with it intact.

CHAPTER 8

THE ZERO ACCOUNTABILITY MAN TRAP

There is a particular species of man roaming the modern dating landscape who believes companionship is something you order à la carte—preferably after 7 p.m., preferably after a drink, and preferably with the option to disappear the moment things require effort, clarity, or pants with buttons.

He is not twenty-two.

That would at least be developmentally coherent. At twenty-two, emotional incoherence is practically a lifestyle choice. A rite of passage. A public service announcement waiting to happen.

No—this man is forty-five.

Sometimes fifty.

Occasionally older.

And yet, emotionally, he is still wearing yesterday's hoodie, scanning the room for pleasure, allergic to depth, and profoundly confused about why women expect… well, anything.

Let us call him the Zero Accountability Man.

You meet him, and within minutes, he begins speaking in euphemisms. Not poetic ones. Not mysterious ones. Lazy ones. Phrases so vague they could double as corporate mission statements.

"I'm just looking to chill."

"I'm very easy-going."

"I go with the flow."

At this point, one must ask: the flow of what, exactly? Gin? Dopamine? Avoidance? The gentle stream of unprocessed childhood wounds?

Because "going with the flow" sounds charming until you realise the flow has no direction, no destination, and no intention beyond immediate gratification and minimal inconvenience.

Example One: The Weekend That Wasn't Romance

One such man—let us call him R- met me for a drink. One drink. A single conversation that barely grazed the surface of who either of us actually was.

Within forty minutes, he leaned back in his chair, smiled with what he clearly believed was effortless charm, and said, "You should come down south for the weekend."

No curiosity about my life. No inquiry into my values. No interest in what I loved, feared, or believed.

Just geography. Logistics. Coordinates.

This, apparently, was intimacy.

When I asked him—calmly, politely—what he actually meant by that, he looked genuinely startled. As though women are meant to accept travel directions as emotional connection.

"Well," demonstrated R, now slightly defensive, "we'll just hang out. No pressure."

Ah yes. The universal red flag phrase. No pressure—which always means all pressure will be silently transferred to you.

"Hang out" involved a vague Airbnb, some alcohol, and the unspoken assumption that my presence itself was consent for whatever he had planned but couldn't be bothered to articulate.

There was no discussion of safety, comfort, intention, or even basic respect. Just the assumption that my time, body, and emotional labour were available on short notice because he had offered a weekend and a vague promise of vibes.

When I declined—politely, again—he was confused. Slightly offended. As though I had rejected not a man, but his version of a diamond ring.

Example Two: The Gin Offering

Another Zero Accountability Man arrived at my home with a bottle of gin and a smile that suggested generosity, maturity, and perhaps even depth.

He placed the bottle down like an offering to the gods.

See? Provision!

See? Effort!

We sat. We talked. Or rather, he talked about himself, his work, his spiritual journey (always a red flag when used as decoration rather than practice), and his belief in "keeping things light."

Eventually, I asked the inevitable question. The question that separates adults from emotionally ambulatory adolescents.

"So… what are you actually looking for?"

He paused. Reflected. Took a sip of gin. And said, with the confidence of a man who has never been asked to explain himself:

"I just want to chill."

Chill!?

At forty-five.

I did not realise adulthood came with a loophole that allowed men to opt out indefinitely while still expecting access to bodies, emotions, laughter, warmth, listening, validation, and sexual availability—on demand.

Apparently, all you need is alcohol, ambiguity, and the audacity to act surprised when women want more than a pleasant evening and an emotional vacuum.

The Core Delusion

This is the central fantasy of the Zero Accountability Man:

He wants the benefits of intimacy without the responsibilities of a relationship.

He wants:

- Emotional access without emotional labour
- Physical closeness without consequence
- Affection without follow-through
- Sex without context
- Connection without coherence

And when things get heavy—when feelings emerge, needs are voiced, or reality intrudes—he disappears.

Not dramatically.

Not honestly.

He vanishes like Casper the Ghost after a casual haunting, leaving behind a faint trail of smoke, confusion, and unread messages.

You are left staring at your phone, replaying conversations, wondering what you said wrong.

But the truth is both brutal and liberating:

You didn't do anything wrong.

You simply crossed the threshold where effort begins.

They Don't Fear Commitment

Let's be clear.

These men do not fear commitment.

They fear accountability.

Accountability requires:

- Presence when it's inconvenient
- Emotional literacy
- Self-reflection
- The ability to tolerate discomfort
- The willingness to repair instead of vanish

The Zero Accountability Man has built an entire personality around avoiding these things.

Alcohol helps.

Casual sex helps.

Vague language helps.

Spiritual jargon sometimes helps ("I'm just being in the now.") I swear some of these men think they are Ekhart Tolle incarnate.

What does not help is a woman who asks clear questions. You will be surprised by how many of these losers I filter out by just a few clear and direct questions-

- What are you looking for? If the answer is vague, you know to stop right there.

- Why are you interested in me? If the answer has something to do with your physical attributes- Run, he only wants you for sex!
- What type of relationship do you envision? Check here for values and goals alignment.

Because clarity exposes the emptiness of the offer.

They speak often of wanting "connection," but what they mean is access. Someone to laugh with them, soothe them, sleep with them, admire them—until the moment the relationship asks them to grow up.

At that point, they become:

- Busy
- Overwhelmed
- Confused
- Unavailable or better yet-
- Triggered

Or worse, they accuse you of being "too intense."

Intensity, apparently, is any expectation beyond "be pleasant and low-maintenance."

The Cultural Gaslight

The most exhausting part is not their immaturity.

It is their conviction that this is normal.

That women are unreasonable for wanting coherence.

That wanting reliability is controlling.

That depth is optional, but sex is essential.

It raises an uncomfortable question:

At what age, exactly, are men meant to grow up?

Or does the teenage self—obsessed with pleasure, novelty, and avoidance—simply get better funding, better vocabulary, and access to better liquor?

Freedom vs. Indulgence

The Zero Accountability Man does not see himself as irresponsible.

He sees himself as "free."

But freedom without responsibility is not freedom.

It is indulgence.

And indulgence, over time, becomes emptiness.

The Real Tragedy

The real tragedy is not that these men exist.

It is that so many women are conditioned to entertain them.

To explain.

To soften.

To negotiate basic adulthood.

The moment you stop doing that—when you stop translating chill into meaning, access into affection, and convenience into companionship—something remarkable happens.

They disappear faster.

And you don't miss them.

Because once you've tasted coherence, the offer of gin, sex, and emotional vacancy feels exactly like what it is:

A bad deal wrapped in confidence.

The Zero Accountability Man is not evil.

He is unfinished.

And women are not rehabilitation centres.

WHY WOMEN FALL FOR THE ZERO ACCOUNTABILITY MAN

(And Why It Has Nothing to Do with Low Standards)

Women do not fall for the Zero Accountability Man because they want less.

They fall because they have been conditioned to make sense of incoherence.

From an early age, many women are trained—explicitly and implicitly—to:

- Be agreeable
- Be flexible
- Be understanding
- Be emotionally fluent
- Be patient with male confusion

So, when a man presents emotional vagueness as a lifestyle choice, women are taught to interpret it generously rather than accurately.

"He's just slow to open up."

"He's been hurt before."

"He's not great with words."

"He's scared of commitment, but he cares."

This is not intuition.

This is cultural translation labour.

1. **The Familiarity of Emotional Under-functioning**
   If a woman grew up around emotionally absent, inconsistent, or avoidant caregivers, the Zero Accountability Man feels strangely familiar. Not exciting—recognisable.
   Her nervous system reads his ambiguity as:
   "This is how connection feels."
   So, she leans in, explains more, softens more, waits longer.
2. **The Illusion of Low Conflict**
   These men often appear calm, easy, and "non-dramatic." To a woman who has survived chaos, this can deceivingly feel like peace.
   But what looks like calm is often emotional absence.
   There is no conflict because there is no investment.
   No tension because nothing is being held.
3. **The False Promise of Potential**
   Zero Accountability Men are masters of almost.
   Almost curious. Almost available. Almost intentional.

They give just enough warmth to keep hope alive, while withholding enough clarity to avoid responsibility. Women fall for who the man could be if he ever decides to show up.

4. **The Internalised Burden of "Being Too Much"**
   Many women have been shamed for wanting clarity, consistency, and depth. So, when a man offers vagueness, she downsizes herself to fit the container.

   She becomes:

   - Less expressive
   - Less demanding
   - Less visible

   She, in turn, becomes small to fit the box.

   Not because she wants to—but because she is trying to be chosen.

5. **The Mislabelling of Avoidance as Independence**
   The Zero Accountability Man frames emotional absence as freedom. Women who value autonomy can mistake this for maturity.

   But independence includes the capacity for real intimacy.

   Avoidance does not.

SOMATIC RED FLAG CHECKLIST

1. **The Vague Offer Sensation**
   In the body: Subtle tightness in the chest or solar plexus
   Red flag behaviour: Plans framed as "we'll see," "let's play it by ear," or last-minute invitations without structure or care
2. **The Clarity Spike**
   In the body: Nervous activation when you ask a simple, adult question

Red flag behaviour: Deflecting, joking, or appearing "overwhelmed" when asked what he wants or can offer

3. **The Shrinking Reflex**

   In the body: Shoulders drop inward; voice softens unnaturally

   Red flag behaviour: You feel the need to downplay your needs, so you don't seem demanding, intense, or difficult

4. **The Aftertaste Check**

   In the body: Emotional flatness or restlessness after time together

   Red flag behaviour: Pleasant interactions that leave no sense of being met, seen, or emotionally nourished

5. **The Translation Fatigue**

   In the body: Mental exhaustion; looping thoughts

   Red flag behaviour: You constantly interpret his words, tone, or silence to find meaning he doesn't clearly provide

6. **The Accountability Aversion**

   In the body: Sudden tension when expectations are named

   Red flag behaviour: He reframes responsibility as pressure, neediness, or control

7. **The Access Imbalance**

   In the body: A sense of over-giving or leaning forward energetically

   Red flag behaviour: He expects emotional warmth, availability, or intimacy without offering consistency or follow-through

8. **The Disappearing Act Response**

   In the body: Drop in energy; hollow or braced feeling

   Red flag behaviour: He becomes busy, distant, or vague after emotional closeness or boundary setting

9. **The "Easy-Going" Alert**
   In the body: Subtle unease masked as calm
   Red flag behaviour: He uses phrases like "no expectations," "keeping it light," or "going with the flow" to avoid commitment
10. **The Settling Test**
   In the body: Inability to fully relax or exhale around him
   Red flag behaviour: Your nervous system never quite lands—because nothing is ever clearly held
   If your nervous system is constantly bracing for clarity that never arrives, you are not in connection—you are in anticipation.

Closing Truth

The Zero Accountability Man does not trap women through deception.

He traps them through absence dressed as ease.

And once your body learns the difference between calm and emptiness, you will never confuse them again.

Let this be a permission slip. To ask clearer questions.

To trust your body's intelligence. To walk away from offers that cost you your steadiness.

When you choose clarity, you do not lose love.

You lose confusion.

And that is not a loss—it is a return.

CHAPTER 9

THE KNOW-IT-ALL ADVICE-GIVING MAN TRAP: OR, CONGRATULATIONS, I DIDN'T ASK

There is a particular kind of man who does not enter a woman's life to meet her.

He arrives to correct her.

He comes armed not with curiosity, but with commentary. Not with desire, but with diagnosis. Within minutes of knowing you, he has identified seventeen things you are doing wrong—your posture, your tone, your diet, your breathing, your laughter, your clothes, your libido, and somehow, your entire nervous system.

Let us call him what he is: The Know-It-All Advice-Giving Man.

He believes his presence alone qualifies him as a consultant. Your life, to him, is an open document begging for edits. Preferably in red ink.

I have encountered so many variations of this man that it could qualify as a research study. From nutrition policing to spiritual micromanagement, from bodily surveillance to behavioural regulation—men have attempted to control and distort every aspect of my being while operating under one core assumption:

I know nothing. They know everything.

What makes this trap especially insidious is that it disguises itself as care.

"I'm just saying this because I care."

"I'm only trying to help."

"I'm being honest."

Honesty, apparently, is a one-way street.

Let's examine three case studies.

Scene One: B — The Wellness Warden

B entered my life with the confidence of a man who had read half a blog post and decided he was now a health authority.

It started innocently.

"You shouldn't eat that."

No hello. No context. Just a verdict.

Apparently, the almonds I was eating were too many. My coffee was too much. My occasional cigarette was toxic. My enjoyment of food was emotional eating. My enjoyment of life was a lack of discipline.

B had opinions about my gut, my hormones, my metabolism, and my future lifespan—none of which he had been invited to comment on.

"Women's bodies are very sensitive," he said, nodding gravely, as though delivering medical wisdom from Mount Sinai.

Ah yes. Sensitive. Fragile. In need of constant male supervision.

What fascinated me was that B's own habits were… flexible. He drank. He slept poorly. He exercised inconsistently. But his body, naturally, was exempt from critique. Male bodies, it seems, are sovereign nations. Female bodies are public property.

At some point, he escalated.

"You shouldn't masturbate so much. It drains energy."

I blinked.

There it was—the audacity fully bloomed. This man, who did not know my body, my libido, my nervous system, or my pleasure, had appointed himself Gatekeeper of My Orgasms.

Let me be clear: when a man attempts to regulate a woman's pleasure, he is not being spiritual. He is being controlling.

This was not a concern. This was colonisation.

B wanted access to my body while simultaneously policing it. Enjoy yourself—but only in ways that don't threaten my authority. Be free—but not wild. Be embodied—but not autonomous.

Eventually, I realised something crucial: B was not uncomfortable with my habits.

He was uncomfortable with my self-trust. My rhythm and my flow with life.

And nothing terrifies a controlling man more than a woman who knows her body better than he ever will.

Scene Two: J — The Posture Police

J was subtler. Politer. More refined in his tyranny.

He didn't tell me what to eat. He told me how to exist.

"Sit straight."

"Don't slouch."

"Breathe deeper."

"Why do you laugh like that?"

"You don't have to speak with so much emphasis."

Every interaction felt like being gently corrected by a disappointed headmaster.

J had a vision of womanhood, and I was failing the audition.

My body, to him, was something to be arranged. My expressions were too much. My voice was too animated. My laughter was too loud. My presence was too alive.

"Calm down," he'd say, when I was perfectly calm.

"You don't have to take up so much space."

Ah. There it is.

This is the heart of the Know-It-All Advice-Giving Man Trap: the discomfort with feminine rhythm.

The feminine is cyclical. Expressive. Wild. It moves. It expands. It contracts. It laughs loudly and speaks passionately and breathes according to feeling, not instruction.

And men like J experience this not as beauty, but as a threat.

So, they attempt to regulate it.

Sit straighter.

Speak softer.

Move less.

Be smaller.

J wasn't trying to help me be better.

He was trying to help himself feel safer.

Because a woman fully at ease in her body does not need permission.

And men who need control cannot tolerate that.

Scene Three: Q — The Aesthetic Authority

Q believed he had excellent taste.

Unfortunately, this belief extended to my wardrobe.

"Why do you wear that?"

"You'd look better if you wore jeans."

"That colour doesn't suit your energy." (He knew nothing of energy).

"Do you always wear bohemian dresses?"

"Men won't take you seriously if you dress like that."

Men. Always men. The invisible jury we are apparently dressing for at all times.

Q had strong opinions about my clothes, my hair, my makeup—or lack thereof. He framed these opinions as guidance, as though I had been wandering the earth tragically underdressed until he arrived to save me.

What made Q especially fascinating was the contradiction at the core of his thinking.

He wanted my wildness.

But not its expression.

He wanted my body.

But not my autonomy.

He wanted access to my emotions, my warmth, my labour, my presence—while simultaneously placing me in a conceptual cage.

Be desirable, but not self-directed. Be sensual, but not sovereign.

Be powerful, but not uncontrollable.

Do you see the irony?

Bind her. Exploit her. Then instruct her on how to behave.

It would be funny if it weren't so common.

What This Trap Really Is

Let us name this behaviour clearly.

This is not advice.

This is not care.

This is disrespect. With a capital D.

It is the assumption that a woman does not know herself. That her body is up for debate. That her choices—personal, professional, physical—are negotiable.

It is the projection of male insecurity dressed up as wisdom.

These men are not confident. They are anxious. They are not grounded. They are threatened. They do not want partnership—they want compliance.

Because a woman who trusts her own rhythm cannot be managed.

And that is the real issue.

A Message to These Men

Take a step back.

Understand this: women know their bodies. We know our pleasure. We know our limits. We know our appetites—physical, emotional, intuitive and intellectual.

You do not get to enter our lives and start issuing instructions.

You do not get to cage us, feed off our resources, our care, our labour—and then dictate how loudly we laugh while doing it.

If you feel the urge to constantly correct a woman, ask yourself this:

What about her freedom unsettles me?

Because the problem is not her posture.

It is your need to dominate.

The Exit

The moment you recognise this trap, something shifts.

You stop explaining. You stop justifying. You stop shrinking.

You let these men talk themselves out of relevance.

Because the Know-It-All Advice-Giving Man does not want a woman.

He wants a project.

And the most radical thing a woman can do is refuse to be one.

Wildness is not a flaw. Autonomy is not arrogance. And unsolicited advice is not wisdom.

It is noise.

And once you stop listening, the silence is glorious.

The Invisible Patriarchy: Five Shadow Patterns of the Know-It-All Advice-Giving Man

This trap is not about individual men.

It is about a system that quietly trains men to mistake dominance for intelligence and authority for care.

This is the invisible patriarchy—not the obvious tyrant, but the well-meaning corrector. The man who believes he is evolved because he "treats women as equals," while subtly assuming he is still the final authority.

Having dated across cultures, continents, and ideologies, I can say this without hesitation: this pattern is global. It wears different accents, but the same psychology.

So, the question is not where it comes from.

The question is: why do so many men believe they know better—and who anointed them gods of reality?

Here are five shadow patterns that answer that.

1. The Inherited Authority Complex

"I speak; therefore, I am right."

From boyhood, men are rewarded for certainty—not wisdom. Confidence, even when hollow, is praised. Questioning oneself is framed as weakness. Listening is optional.

By adulthood, this calcifies into an unconscious belief:

My perception is more accurate than yours.

When this man meets a woman—especially an intuitive, embodied, emotionally literate one—his nervous system does not register her knowing as intelligence. It registers it as competition.

So, he advises. He Corrects. He explains- also known as mansplaining.

Not because he knows more—but because he was never taught to trust knowledge that doesn't sound like his own voice.

2. The Disowned Womb

Men forget they came from a woman.

This is the deepest shadow.

Men are born from the womb, nourished by a woman's body, regulated by her nervous system—then spend a lifetime distancing themselves from that origin.

Why?

Because patriarchy teaches men that:

- The womb is chaotic
- The feminine is irrational
- The body is inferior to the mind

So instead of honouring the source, they dominate it.

The advice-giving man unconsciously attempts to outgrow his origin by asserting control over women—especially over their bodies, instincts, pleasure, and choices.

It is not superiority. It is separation trauma.

3. The False Feminist Shadow

"I respect women—as long as they agree with me."

This man believes he is progressive.

He listens. He uses the right language. He supports "strong women."

Until she disagrees.

Until she doesn't take his advice. Until she doesn't adjust herself to his worldview.

Then the mask slips.

Equality, to him, means:

You are equal as long as you don't challenge my authority.

He cannot tolerate a woman who is sovereign rather than collaborative, self-trusting rather than seeking consensus.

So, he advises her "for her own good."

This is not feminism. This is control with better branding.

4. The Anxiety-to-Authority Conversion

Uncertainty converted into instruction.

Men are not taught how to sit with not knowing.

So, when faced with:

- A woman's emotional depth
- Her intuitive decisions
- Her nonlinear rhythms

Their nervous system spikes.

And instead of saying:

"I don't understand."

They say: "Here's what you should do."

Advice becomes a way to regulate THEIR discomfort.

This is why the advice often arrives when it is not requested.

Because it is not in her best interest.

It is for his relief.

5. The God-Given Authority Myth

No one gave it to them. They took it.

There is no divine council. No universal mandate. No cosmic memo that says men know better.

This authority is self-appointed.

It is upheld by repetition, not truth.

By entitlement, not wisdom.

And the moment a woman stops accepting it—

The moment she doesn't explain, justify, or comply—

The illusion collapses.

Why Women Fall for This Trap: The Self-Worth Mirror

This is the part that requires brutal honesty—with compassion.

Women do not fall for this trap because they are naïve.

They fall for it because self-worth has not yet fully landed in the body.

You see, our partners are mirrors—not of who we are, but of what we believe we deserve.

If you are a diamond but feel like coal, you will negotiate for coal and call it love.

Women who fall for the Advice-Giving Man often carry one or more of these imprints:

- They were praised for being "the good girl," not for being sovereign
- Their intuition was questioned early in life
- Love was conditional on being agreeable
- Authority figures knew better than their inner voice

So, when a man arrives who seems confident, directive, certain—it can feel like safety.

But guidance without consent is not love.

A woman who has not yet fully claimed her worth may mistake being managed for being chosen.

Until one day, her body speaks louder than her conditioning.

The Somatic Red Flag Checklist

Ten Body-Based Signals You're in the Advice-Giving Man Trap

Read this slowly. Let your body answer before your mind does.

Ask yourself:

1. Do I feel smaller after sharing something vulnerable with him?
   Not challenged. Smaller.
2. Does my chest subtly tighten when he starts "helping"?
   That's your heart closing.
3. Do I feel the urge to explain myself more around him?
   Over-explaining is a trauma response.
4. When he gives advice, do I feel interrupted—even if he's calm?
   Interruption isn't about volume. It's about overriding.
5. Does my breath become shallow when he corrects me?
   Your nervous system knows before your mind does.
6. Do I feel less confident in the choices I was perfectly fine with before meeting him?
   This is energetic erosion.
7. When I share joy or excitement, does he "ground" it instead of celebrating it?
   Joy suppression is control.
8. Do I feel watched rather than witnessed?

Surveillance is not intimacy.

9. When I don't take his advice, does he become subtly withdrawn, irritated, or superior?
   Conditional approval is a leash.
10. After interacting with him, do I need to self-soothe?
    Love should regulate—not drain—you.

Final body question:

Does my heart expand—or brace—around him?

Your body does not lie. It has never lied. It has only been overridden.

Closing Truth

The Advice-Giving Man does not want your growth.

He wants your compliance.

And the moment you stop needing his approval, his authority evaporates.

A woman who trusts her body is ungovernable. She honours her own rhythms and intuitive flow.

A woman who listens to her nervous system cannot be colonised.

A woman who knows her worth does not argue with noise.

She simply walks away.

And that—

That is liberation.

CHAPTER 10

THE TURNING POINT — THE PSYCHOPATHIC PATHOLOGICAL LIAR MAN TRAP

Let's be clear about the world we live in today- the age of scams.

Emotional scams, spiritual scams, love scams. Men and women alike have weaponised loneliness and turned it into a fish market of games. They sell illusion- packaged love, borrowed empathy, and manufactured intimacy — all for money, sex, or power.

This story is about one such man.

Let's call him A.

The Setup: A Mirage of Opportunity

At the time, my life felt like it was collapsing. My job as a communications and content writer at a so-called "conscious community" was unravelling because I had dared to question the hypocrisy within. Sometimes I truly wonder: was I ever meant to just "do my job," or have I been placed on Earth to clear up spaces of injustice and unsafety for women?

That's when A entered the picture.

He reached out, dangling what seemed like a golden opportunity- to head the Dance Movement Therapy program at NIMHANS.

He claimed he had already spoken to a director there and was "in discussions" about my role. He spoke with such detail and confidence that I almost believed he was my destiny-ordained bridge back into purpose.

But something felt off.

He never once included me in any call with this so-called director.

My intuition- that quiet pulse of knowing- kept tugging at me. But I ignored it, because he listened to me. Hours on end. I was starved for a genuine emotional connection. And just that was enough.

The Unravelling: Gaslighting and Guilt

One day, he left his phone open.

No WhatsApp chats. No calls. No trace of this "director."

When I confronted him, that's when the first gaslight hit. He flipped the narrative with masterful precision- "You don't trust me. You have boundary issues. You need healing."

He cried on cue, played fragile, even invoked illness to shift my focus. I remember thinking- he could win an Oscar. He performed pain like an art form. He feigned love to lure the vulnerable on cue. Within 3 days, he generated a message from the director with many spelling and grammatical errors and sent a screenshot to me. I had every reason to believe this was generated by him, yet I chose to trust him because I was desperate and hopeful for some solution out of the environment I was in. Of course, no interview for that job was set up. No confirmation, zero accountability. Every time I had to receive anything tangible from him, it always became more about him being the victim.

Then came the next hook: "I'm in the hospital," he said, breathless, "I can't breathe… asthma attacks, spasms."

I began cooking for him, taking food to him, even giving him Reiki on the streets. I did all this even when there was a struggle for resources of the help's time and effort at my own family home. Growing up in a traditional Bengali joint family, I'd seen this pattern- women always serving first, eating last. It was the quiet conditioning that women exist to feed others, not themselves, after being the nourishers themselves. It was for generations that women had perpetuated these deranged patterns of babying the men. Without realising it, I was reliving that script- yet again.

The Exploitation

Soon, A began asking for money. First for his medication, then for his stay at various hostels and Airbnb. I found it odd that a man who claimed to have held an esteemed job at a mental health initiative, having so many "so-called" contacts, had not found a place to stay long-term. But he totally cornered me into asking deep questions about fundamental things like background, family dynamics, etc. The family was apparently evil, and he was the so-called saint who could do no wrong.

He promised repayment once his "inheritance came through." Which, later, I realised was yet another carrot, another hook to reel me in.

Weeks turned into months. The inheritance never came.

Instead, I had panic attacks, sleepless nights, and his trademark manipulation- "You're stressing me out, my blood pressure's 170 because of you." He was the one causing me anxiety, but instead I was somehow apologising and begging for my own money, my dignity. Every attempt I made to set boundaries was flipped into guilt.

He claimed to be the one offering me emotional safety while he was systematically draining my finances, resources, energy, and spirit. Preying on my soft, nurturing and trusting heart.

The brutal truth was that I had fallen for a parasite- a man who survived by feeding on the life force and resources of others.

The Dream and The Revelation

Then one morning at 6:30 a.m., I had a dream so vivid it felt prophetic. What he underestimated in me was how divinely protected I truly am. Before any major loss, financial or physical, could occur, this dream woke me up to his truth.

I was in a filthy train station, waiting with my bags packed. Dying fish were scattered across the ground. Stray cats circled. Fat men ogling. I waited for A- forty minutes, maybe more- before realising he had vanished.

When I called him, he had blocked me.

And what played next felt like a nightmare leaking into daylight- a deranged semblance of his voice recording:

"Sex, sex, sex- that's all you think about, you fake healer. I'm with my sugar baby. I spent your money on her. She's on her period. Come clean it. That's all you're good for."

I woke up with a piercing pain in my chest. That's when my heart shattered.

I called him in disbelief- and he reacted as though I was accusing him. As if it were the truth, and on many levels it was.

That was the moment I knew: this was divine intervention.

When I spoke to our mutual contact- a man running a mental health support group- the truth poured out.

This parasite had a pattern.

He preyed on vulnerable women by luring them in through by feigning empathy. He had preyed on numerous women in this mental health support group. Women who were susceptible to breakdowns, even suicide. But did he care? Not a damn! He was exploiting them primarily for money, some for sex and then inviting call girls to the places he wanted to stay. Yes! On their dime. My contact even told me that he was almost certain my money had gone to some call girls satiating his desires.

He spoke fluent "trauma language," knew just enough psychology to mimic care. He faked credentials, inflated roles, and destroyed lives. My story was just another in his string of manipulations.

The Realisation: The Dark Mirror

It took a week to separate truth from fiction. I realised that A had weaponised my trauma- my softness, my need to heal- against me.

He told me he respected my boundaries and would only offer "emotional intimacy." But what he actually did was far worse.

He raped my mind, heart, and soul. He spun a web of lies with such bravado and precision- it almost felt as if he believed his own bullshit. This was no delusion or psychosis- this was lies that served a purpose- his own dubious needs. This man had even deceived his psychiatrist in providing him a disability card- which was his get out of jail free card.

And yet- this was my turning point.

The Alchemy of Awakening

In studying what had happened, I discovered something profound:

The same trauma that creates an empath can also create a narcissist- even a psychopath.

These are two sides of the same wound.

A narcissist is drawn to an empath's light like a moth to a flame- not for warmth, but for consumption. What the empath experiences as divine connection is often just her own love mirrored back- until the illusion breaks.

The Signs of a Psychopathic Pathological Liar- The Shadow Side

1. Makes grandiose, unbelievable claims with zero evidence.
2. Uses digital or fabricated proof (AI chats, videos, screenshots).
3. Begins with intense affection- classic love bombing.
4. Plays victim when confronted.
5. Weaponises guilt and emotions.
6. Twists reality until you doubt your sanity.
7. Exploits your deepest wounds and fears.
8. Labels you as unstable or unlovable to regain control.

The Patterns I Had to Heal

1. Overextending to earn love- performing for affection.
2. Mistaking basic empathy for emotional intimacy.
3. Trusting too quickly, ignoring my intuition even when my gut was reacting very early on.
4. Believing "evil" only exists in stories.

Becoming the Sovereign Empath

Through this fire, I learned true discernment.

I learned that love without boundaries is self-betrayal.

That empathy must be balanced with wisdom.

That compassion without discernment is not kindness- it's self-abandonment.

A sovereign empath learns this the hard way.

She becomes the weapon- not to harm, but to protect her own light.

She knows when to hold compassion and when to wield the sword.

My takeaways were simple yet sacred:

My love is precious and rare- it must be earned.

My heart is not a charity- it's a temple.

I will never again feed parasites-only nourish equals.

From that day on, I crowned myself the Empress of My Own Heart.

And I turned the love I once gave away recklessly — back toward myself.

The Somatic Checklist: When the Story Doesn't Add Up but Your Body Already Knows

Psychopathic pathological liars do not collapse reality all at once.

They spin it slowly, counting on one thing: that you will override your gut in favour of hope.

This checklist is not intellectual. It is somatic.

Because the body detects deception long before the mind has language for it.

Read each point and notice what happens in your chest, belly, throat, and spine.

1. **Your stomach tightens when they speak — even when the words are "kind."**
   This is not anxiety. This is incongruence. Your body is registering a mismatch between tone and truth.
2. **Their stories are detailed — but never verifiable.**
   Names without faces.
   Positions without proof.
   Opportunities without emails, calls, or shared spaces.
   Your body senses the missing weight of reality.
3. **You are never introduced to real people from their lives.**
   No family.
   No long-term friends.
   No one can corroborate history.
   Isolation is not accidental — it is confinement.
4. **You feel subtly disoriented after conversations.**
   Not confused — off-centre.
   Like reality shifted half an inch to the left.
   This is early-stage gaslighting, and your nervous system feels it first.
5. **Every question you ask turns into an emotional emergency.**
   Curiosity is reframed as cruelty.
   Accountability becomes "pressure."
   Your body learns that asking equals danger — and begins to shut down.

6. **Your chest feels heavy when you think of confronting them.**
   This is not fear of conflict.
   This is your heart recognising that truth is unsafe in their presence.
7. **You begin managing their emotions at the cost of your own stability.**
   Your body enters caretaker mode, even when you are depleted.
   This is not love — it is trauma replay.
8. **You feel urgency without clarity.**
   Everything must happen now.
   Money, help, commitment, trust — immediately.
   Urgency is the enemy of discernment, and your body resists it.
9. **You start doubting sensations you used to trust.**
   Your intuition speaks — and is immediately overridden by their explanation.
   Each time you silence yourself, your body registers self-betrayal.
10. **The Closing Truth — Your Body Sounds the Alarm Early**
    Here is the most important truth of this entire chapter:
    Your body warned you.
    Every single time.
    The tight chest.
    The nausea.
    The fatigue after contact.
    The early "something is off" that you couldn't explain.
    You did not miss the signs.

You overrode them — because you were conditioned to prioritise empathy over truth, hope over evidence, compassion over self-protection.
The cost of overriding your gut is always paid in the body first —
and in resources, dignity, and safety later.

The Final Takeaway: Trust Your Gut or Pay the Price

This chapter exists for one reason only:

To say this, without dilution or softness:

Your intuition is not poetic. It is not spiritual flair. It is not trauma.

It is biological intelligence.

My body sounded the alarm early.

I felt it in my chest. In my sleep. In my breath.

And I ignored it — because I wanted to believe.

Because I was tired. Because I needed hope.

And I paid the price — emotionally, somatically, financially.

Let this be the line that ends the chapter and begins your sovereignty:

If the story doesn't add up, it's because it isn't true.

If your body is uneasy, it's because it knows.

And no opportunity, no saviour, no wounded man is worth betraying your gut.

Empathy without discernment feeds predators. Love without boundaries invites parasites.

But a woman who trusts her body? She is unscammable. She is unreachable.

She is sovereign.

And that is the turning point.

CHAPTER 11

AN INNER REFLECTION- THE WOUNDS IN ME THAT MAGNETISED UNHEALED MEN

I grew up carrying both the mother wound and the father wound, twin inheritances that carved themselves into my psyche long before I had language for any of it. I was the overachiever, the bright flame in a household slowly dimming, until my father's business collapsed in 2017 and something darker seemed to awaken in him. His health failed, but instead of seeking healing, he funnelled every shard of his rage, shame, and unprocessed grief onto me. It was as if a demonic force possessed him—he would hurl insults sharp enough to slice through bone, goading me, provoking me, lighting a match and then recoiling in false innocence when the fire rose. And rise it did. Kali's rage—the ancient, volcanic force buried in generations of silenced women—erupted through me. I fought back, not because I wanted to, but because something primal and sacred refused annihilation. Meanwhile, my mother—once an educated lawyer with her own dreams—had become a submissive, covert narcissist, a woman who traded her voice for survival and dissolved into denial. She lived in the haze of overeating, oversleeping, and avoiding life itself, hiding in a body she no longer lived in. She never intervened when my father and I went to war; she stood silent, watching, embodying everything I refused to become. And in that battlefield of contradictions—between a father who despised my fire and a mother who feared her own—I was forged into the opposite of them: a woman who could no longer be silenced, shamed, or controlled. Every action has an equal and opposite reaction — Newton whispered a truth that applies as much to physics as it does to love.

Because what we attract is not random.

It's gravitational.

It's energetic.

And it's predictable if you know the fault lines inside yourself.

For years, my unhealed places were not quiet shadows; they were loud sirens. They were broadcasting my wounds into the world like a beacon. And the men who found me were not partners — they were mirrors, each one reflecting a different fracture.

Here's the thing I didn't want to admit for a long time: My voids chose my relationships before I did. My patterns were simple, ancient, and devastating:

1. A hunger for attention and validation

Not the superficial kind — the "see me, hear me, choose me, don't leave" kind.

The kind born when a child grows up raising her mother instead of being held by her. Silenced by neglect and abuse. Yes, provided for financially, but starving and thirsting for love, adoration and care.

So, what did I do? The screaming wounds in me attracted all the types of dysfunctions that were humanly possible. You've seen it in my relationships.

The way I mistook their temporary tenderness as permanent safety.

The way avoidance made me chase harder, thinking I could earn consistency from inconsistency.

2. A crippling fear of abandonment

When love was present, it felt like air. When it was absent, I felt like I couldn't breathe.

So, I tolerated more than I should have. I forgave faster than healing allowed. I romanticised breadcrumbs, mistaking them for a feast.

Remember the flaksters?

The men who mirrored commitment but delivered nothing? They knew exactly how to feed the abandonment wound — a little attention, a little fantasy, a little touch —and suddenly my nervous system was hooked like it was a survival requirement.

3. The slide into co-dependency

Co-dependency doesn't start with weakness. It starts with over-functioning strength. I was always the giver. The healer. The holder of pain. The one who tried to rescue emotionally unavailable men from themselves, hoping they'd love me for the effort.

Whether it was the man who oscillated between warmth and cruelty, or the ones who loved the idea of me but not the responsibility of loving me, I kept shrinking so they could feel big enough to stay.

The flip-side of co-dependency is a theory I have- "The Damsel in Distress Theory." I have seen this time and time again within myself. When I am in a relationship, I become co-dependent and need care-taking- this perpetuates my own unhealed patterns and further feeds a toxic dynamic far longer than it should go on. Remember the time I stayed on in my abusive marriage for the cuddling privileges? It seems so ridiculous now, but at the time that was my lifeline. My question here is- why do women crumble when in a relationship? Why do we lose ourselves? The urge here is to be interdependent; to be whole and to attract wholeness.

4. Ego chemistry disguised as destiny

Let's talk about the spiritual loophole. When I felt "chemistry," it was usually not soul recognition —It was wound recognition.

My anxious attachment met their avoidant attachment, and the spark felt volcanic. But that volcano wasn't passion. It was trauma reenactment disguised as fate. This is why Z felt divine. Not because he was. But because our wounds were karmic twins. When he triggered me, it felt like electricity. When he soothed me, it felt like salvation. I confused regulation with romance. Intensity with intimacy. Chaos with connection.

5. The rescuer complex

Every "broken" man felt like a project my heart wanted to fix:

- the ones who wanted sex but called it "exploring"
- the ones who ghosted and returned like it was their birthright
- the ones who were emotionally volatile
- the spiritually bypassed men who spoke of consciousness but couldn't regulate themselves
- the men who loved my light but not my power

I kept believing I could heal them into loving me. As if love were something I could earn. As if devotion were a reward for emotional labour.

But the truth is: Every man I tried to save needed to be released, not rescued.

6. And beneath all of this? One truth:

I had abandoned myself long before any man did. I abandoned myself every time I ignored the red flags. Every time, I justified their inconsistency. Every time their needs became bigger than my sense of self. Every time I dimmed my fire to keep the peace.

Every time I believed love was something to chase. And as long as I kept abandoning myself, I kept attracting men who did the same.

The Turning Point

When I finally understood this — really understood it — something snapped.

Not my heart.

My pattern.

Because the truth is, I wasn't attracting wounded men because they were powerful.

I attracted them because I was powerful — and they fed on my light like moths finding a flame.

The day I stopped abandoning myself was the day:

- The flaksters disappeared
- The avoidants lost access
- The manipulators lost control
- The karmic mirrors broke
- The trauma bonds dissolved
- My energy stopped leaking
- My sovereignty returned

CHAPTER 12

SOVEREIGNTY & INTEGRATION

The Sovereign Empath

A century ago, Carl Jung wrote about a rare breed of empaths—those who were not simply sensitive, but forged. These were not the soft-edged, wide-open, bleeding-hearted empaths we romanticise today; these were empaths who had survived fire after fire, betrayal after betrayal, narcissist after narcissist. Jung saw them as anomalies in the human psyche, the ones who—when pushed beyond what any psyche should tolerate—either collapsed entirely or awakened into something else.

Something dangerous.

Something sovereign.

For every empath who breaks under systemic narcissistic abuse, there is another who rises with a clarity so sharp it slices deception before it reaches them. That is the crossroads Jung spoke of without naming it directly: the empath either dissolves or evolves.

The one who dissolves becomes a sponge—absorbing everyone's pain, losing their own voice, drowning in borrowed emotions. They become reactive, volatile, and exhausted. They become food for predators.

But the one who evolves?

The one who walks through the final betrayal and does not die?

She becomes Sovereign.

She becomes a weapon the narcissist never anticipated—an empath who now sees.

She reads energy before words. She detects manipulation before seduction. She calls out patterns before they take root. She meets compassion with compassion, but deceit with a blade of truth. She becomes a radar in a world of duality—where love and cruelty coexist, where intention is currency, where innocence is often prey.

People like us have been fed the comforting lie that "everyone is love," that "everyone is one," that "we all have intuition and goodness inside." And yes—at the level of the soul, perhaps that is true. But here, in this dimension, we live in a world where free will can be used to harm just as easily as to heal.

Intelligence can be used to comfort or to conquer. Charm can be used to seduce or to deceive. Love can be used to nourish or to trap.

Every soul arrives at a crossroads. Every person chooses their orientation.

Mine came disguised as betrayal.

Not the soft heartbreaks of adolescence, not the wounding of early relationships—but a betrayal so seismic that it split my psyche, my body, my intuition, and my soul all at once. It was the kind of betrayal that should have ended me. It was the kind of rupture that pushes most empathic women into years of spiralling, numbing, collapsing.

But the divine rerouted me. It was not a whisper. It was an echo. It reverberated through my bones:

Rise. Remember who you are. Take the throne. And so, I did.

I realised I could do everything I was taught to seek in a man. I could provide. I could protect. I could create. I could love. I could nurture.

I became whole not because someone loved me, but because someone left me—and in the wreckage I found all the pieces of myself I had abandoned to maintain connection.

I understood a truth women have been conditioned to forget: My spirit is lightest when it is free. My heart is fullest when it belongs to me. My life is richest when I am the author, not the subordinate.

I realised the madness of seeking validation from men who borrow our softness but never return safety. I realised how often women contort—shrinking, bending, shrinking some more—to fit into a man-child's emotional limitations. I realised how often we are taught to soothe their wounds while they deepen ours.

Because here is the truth no one wants to say aloud: Most men are not taught to hold the feminine; they are taught to consume her. To feed on her emotional vulnerability. To extract devotion without earning trust. To take softness without offering safety. To worship her beauty while resenting her power.

And then they call it love.

But real masculine energy has nothing to do with domination. It is presence. It is stillness. It is the unwavering container that lets the feminine expand, create, and thrive.

Yet most men have not cultivated this.

And instead of admitting their fragility, their fears, their shame—they weaponise our vulnerabilities, twist and project their wounding, ultimately marking our deepest lessons.

They manipulate, gaslight, seduce, extract, and abandon. They leave women bleeding and then call them "too emotional." Tell me, where did men learn these tactics? I would like to truly understand where a narcissist gets their training. There was a time I was dealing with 3 narcissists all at once- at work and at home. They all exhibited the same or very similar patterns.

So let me ask the forbidden question:

Are men evolving towards becoming unnecessary and completely redundant? Are they forcing women into such extreme self-reliance that women will eventually stop seeking them altogether?

Because in a world where women now protect themselves, provide for themselves, heal themselves, create for themselves, and carry spiritual intelligence that many men refuse to cultivate, what exactly are men offering?

If the masculine refuses to rise, the feminine will rise alone.

And when she rises alone, she becomes unstoppable.

When she rises alone, she becomes sovereign.

The journey of the Sovereign Empath is not gentle.

It is not pretty. It is not poetic.

It is a war cry. It is the moment she says ENOUGH.

It is the moment she takes the reins, the sword, and the throne. It is the moment her princess tiara turns into a crown of jagged thorns, adorning all the wounds she had to endure to come to this point.

It is the moment men who once fed on her softness become irrelevant.

This is not misandry. This is evolution.

This is the chapter of the empath who did not break. But rose, beyond that which tried to tame her.

My Gratitude Ode- The Ones Who Carried Me to Shore

People often ask how I survived.

How a child raised on a battlefield of neglect and emotional abandonment, a young woman thrust into an abusive marriage, and then a soul thrust into relationship after relationship that scorched instead of soothed, that used and abused- how she continued to rise when everything around her tried to turn her into ash.

What sustained me? What kept me breathing when life felt like a series of fires designed to burn me to the ground?

The truth is this:

I was never walking alone. Yes, I am strong- forged in heat, refined in darkness, sharpened by pain. But even iron needs something to cool it. Even fire needs something to hold it.

And life, in its strange and sacred compassion, gave me exactly that.

The first force that carried me was Kali- not as a deity on an altar but as a living current inside my spine. She was the presence who stood behind me in every confrontation when my voice trembled. She was the force that rose inside me when my father's rage tried to dismantle my spirit. She was the fire in my belly every time a man tried to manipulate, gaslight, or diminish me. It was her flames that refused to let me collapse.

Kali did not just protect me- She awakened me. She taught me that destruction is also a form of creation. That the breaking was, in fact, the awakening.

But the second guardian, the one who walked beside me in flesh and breath, was my Shihtzu- Tinanz. Tinanz is not just a pet.

He is a living embodiment of unconditional love.

A soul that did not ask, demand, or take — only mirrored, absorbed, and protected. His devotion is so fierce that he would fall sick when I was hurting, as though his tiny body chose to absorb the fire so mine wouldn't have to. When anxiety surged through me, it surged through him. When I froze, he froze. When I rose, he rose with me.

He is my grounding, my compass, my anchor in a world that felt too sharp, too loud, too cruel. He saw me when no one else did. He mirrored my soul when even I couldn't recognise myself. He is the guardian and keeper of my inner child. He kept my joy, lightness and love intact.

And then, there was the other feminine.

The quiet, unacknowledged, overlooked feminine- the women who came into my life not as mothers by blood but as mothers by destiny.

My nannies. My helpers. My caretakers. My unexpected angels.

Women who the world dismisses as "uneducated," yet carry more instinct, tenderness, and maternal intelligence than my own mother ever did. They were attuned to my hunger, my fatigue, my moods, my rhythms. They knew when to feed me, when to soothe me, when to sit beside me without words.

They loved me in the ways I had never been loved. They nurtured me with a purity that asked for nothing in return. They felt like home when home felt like a battlefield.

I bonded with them deeply- because my soul recognised what my body had longed for since childhood: mothering.

Not the biological kind, but the divine kind. The kind that comes from spirit, not DNA. The kind that arrives when the universe refuses to let a child go unloved. These were the boats that carried me through the tunnel. These were the hands that pulled me out of the fire when I was too exhausted to crawl. These were the souls that the universe sent to remind me I was worthy of tenderness, worthy of protection, worthy of being held.

And so, when I look back, I don't see a girl who survived alone.

I see a girl who was carried by love in its most unexpected forms- a goddess, a dog, and a lineage of women who came in as quiet angels.

This is my gratitude, etched into the pages of my becoming: Thank you to everything and everyone who held me when the world tried to break me. Thank you for loving me out of survival. Thank you for walking me to shore.

CHAPTER 13

EMBODYING THE INNER SACRED UNION

There is a point in the Shiv–Shakti myth that is rarely spoken about—the moment before union, when power erupts without containment, when Shakti remembers herself but has not yet been met by Shiva's stillness. That is the stage I lived.

For years, I existed in the shadow aspect of devotion. I over-gave. I bent. I disappeared in relationships, confusing endurance with love and self-erasure with spirituality. Like Sati in her first incarnation, I tried to belong in spaces that could not honour my truth. I absorbed, accommodated, tolerated—until my body and soul reached a breaking point.

And then Kali awoke. Not gently. Not symbolically.

Volcanically.

This was not the romanticised Kali of Instagram art and poetic metaphors. This was raw, embodied rage—ancestral, cellular, unstoppable. After my awakening, something primal erupted in me. Every broken dynamic, every boundary crossed, every subtle dismissal ignited fury. My nervous system lived on a hair trigger. My voice rose to decibels I didn't recognise as my own. My body shook when I was angry—not from weakness, but from power that had been suppressed for too long.

This is the phase most women are taught to fear.

But in mythology, this is not pathology—it is necessary destruction.

Kali emerges when Shakti has been violated one time too many times. She is the refusal to be consumed again. She cuts through illusion, through politeness, through spiritual bypassing. In me, Kali arrived to say: Enough! Enough dilution. Enough disappearance. Enough love without reciprocity.

Yet Kali alone cannot be the destination.

Because while rage liberates, it also burns the vessel that holds it.

There came a point where I realised my body could not sustain the constant fire. I was no longer being oppressed by others—I was being consumed by the very force that had saved me. In the myths, Kali's dance threatens to destroy the cosmos itself until Shiva intervenes. He lies beneath her feet, not to dominate her, but to ground her.

My Shiva did not arrive as a man. He arrived as space.

When I moved into my own home—into my own energy—something fundamental shifted. I lived alone, with my dog, at the intersection of nature and civilisation. Trees outside my window. Silence inside my nervous system. For the first time, my body began to unwind. The hypervigilance softened. My breath deepened. My rage no longer needed to scream to be heard.

This was Shiva's stillness walking beside me.

In the myth, Shiva is not passive. He is containment itself—the infinite witness that allows Shakti's power to exist without destroying itself. As my life became more self-governed, something miraculous happened: forgiveness returned. Compassion resurfaced—not as self-sacrifice, but as choice.

I ran my own house. I held my own structure. I even supported my parents—but through healthy boundaries, not depletion. I could say yes without resentment and no without guilt. I was no longer oscillating between collapse and explosion. I was contained.

And then the symbolism began appearing uninvited.

A Shivlingam stone was placed in my path. Flowers associated with Shiva arriving unexpectedly.

Moments of profound stillness after years of inner chaos.

The containment I had once desperately sought in men—the steady presence, the grounding, the emotional reliability—had come from within me.

This is the forgotten teaching of the Shiv–Shakti myth. The sacred union is not something you wait for externally. It is something you become.

Shakti without Shiva is chaos.

Shiva without Shakti is lifelessness.

But together, within the same being, they create wholeness.

I began to feel it in my body: a balanced masculine and feminine energy coexisting. My inner masculine—once outsourced to partners—now lived in my spine, my routines, my capacity to hold myself. My inner feminine—once wounded and over-giving—now flowed freely, creatively, sensually, without fear of annihilation.

This was not the suppression of Kali. Kali was honoured. Integrated. She no longer needed to scream because she was no longer ignored.

In the Sati–Kali–Parvati arc, this is the final return: Shakti reincarnates not as sacrifice, not as rage alone, but as sovereign partnership. She chooses Shiva again—not because she needs him to complete her, but because she is whole.

That is where I stand now. Compassionate yet contained. Powerful yet grounded. Devotional without self-erasure.

I do not need a man to provide stillness. I am the stillness. I do not fear my rage. It served its purpose. I do not abandon my softness. It is now protected.

This is what it means to live the Shiv–Shakti myth—not as a story, but as a nervous system reality. To let Kali burn what is false. To let Shiva hold what is true. And to allow the sacred marriage to occur within, so that no external relationship is ever asked to do the work of inner union again.

This is not enlightenment.

It is embodiment.

The Two Destinies of the Soul

Two Paths of Enlightenment

In every lifetime, the soul stands at a fork in its evolution. Not all awakening looks like saffron robes, Himalayan caves, or renunciation. Some enlightenment happens in the kitchen, in the bedroom, in the boardroom, in the wreckage of a breakup, in the quiet fury of self-betrayal, or in the triumphant moment you finally reclaim your power.

There are at least two ancient, sacred roads:

The Path of Detachment — The Monk's Ascent

To loosen the grip of desire. To step away from human chaos. To dissolve into silence, stillness, and the arms of the Divine.

Awakening here is a soft, clean fire — the steady flame of those who choose solitude as their teacher.

The Path of Union — The Lover's Descent

To stay. To feel. To break open. To confront every shadow that relationships drag up from the unconscious.

Here, enlightenment is alchemical. It is earned through devotion, conflict, heartbreak, and the courageous rebuilding of the Self.

This path is not for the faint-hearted.

It is awakening through intensity — through the mirror of another, through karmic loops, through ancestral and generational trauma, through love that wounds and love that resurrects.

And if you choose this path, know this truth: Two wounded souls do not create a sacred union. They create karmic lessons. They come to shake you awake. To expose your unmet needs. To initiate your power. To push you toward yourself.

Only when you become your own home — emotionally, mentally, spiritually — does the Divine Union become possible.

What does conscious partnership look like?

- Safety that regulates your nervous system
- Trust that doesn't need constant testing
- Respect that honours your boundaries
- Love that amplifies your life force — never dims it
- Two complete beings choosing each other freely
- Zero need for validation
- Two sovereign flames dancing the cosmic dance

This is now Dharmic relating. Their very union accelerates the universal frequency. That is the power of their love. It doesn't arrive to fill each other's voids. Not to rescue or fix. But to expand the universe together.

This is not performative "consciousness" of minimalism, eating millets, and moral superiority. This is the real thing — the merging of two awakened energies.

My Path Chose Me

For a long time, I oscillated between these worlds. My soul craved freedom. My human self craved love, validation, and safety. For decades, there was a war between the hermit in me and the lover in me. But awakening doesn't happen when you resolve the war. It happens when you become the one who watches it. And that is what happened to me. Today, I stand fully in my higher self—anchored, sovereign, unshakeable. I do not seek love.

I am love.

I am fire.

I am the flame that once searched for warmth outside, not knowing she was the source.

I am open to partnership, but not obligated to it.

I welcome union, but only if it aligns with the sovereignty I bled to earn.

This is my path: The Path of Union — transmuted into Sovereignty.

It broke me open, burned me down, rebuilt me, and crowned me.

And Now I Ask You…Which destiny is your soul writing in this lifetime?

The silence of the mountain? Or the fire of the marketplace?

Neither is superior. Both lead home.

What Path Is Calling You?

Maybe, like me, you'll find yourself oscillating between the mountaintop and the marketplace — between detachment and union — learning that both are teachers and neither is a mistake.

Because perhaps, just perhaps, the soul knows exactly what it's doing. Some relationships arrive as karmic chisels. They carve you open, sculpt your strength, sharpen your intuition, and temper you in fire until you become the sovereign sword you were always meant to be.

And once the blade is forged — once you stand in your truth without apology — the dharmic relationship arrives.

Not to complete you, but to walk beside you. So yes, today I have zero tolerance for anything that falls below my standards, below my embodiment, below my integrity.

Not out of bitterness — but out of clarity. Not out of fear — but out of devotion to my own soul. Yet my heart remains hopeful. And that hope is not naïve. It is the mark of an optimist, a mystic, a lover of the Divine.

For a woman who walks in truth is never truly alone; even when no human walks beside her, the Divine does. This is not confusion. This is alignment. This is trust.

This is the soft, luminous certainty that love — real love — comes when the soul is ready, not when the ego is lonely.

And always, she walks with the Divine, with or without her mate.

What Is Conscious Relating?

In today's world, intimacy is everywhere, and connection is rare.

We live inside a body buffet—endless swipes, open containers, borrowed language of devotion, borrowed language of tantra, borrowed language of healing. Desire is easy. Access is easy. Even spiritual vocabulary is easy now. It can be learned, mimicked, and weaponised.

What is not easy is conscious relating. Conscious relating is not chemistry. Chemistry is hormones and memory and familiarity firing at once. It is not intensity. Intensity is nervous-system activation that mistakes urgency for meaning. It is not a shared language about growth, trauma, or spirituality. Those are just words. And words, as many women have learned the hard way, are cheap.

Conscious relating is something far quieter. And because it is quiet, it is often overlooked. Conscious relating begins with containment, not consumption.

In unconscious dynamics, people enter relationships hungry. Hungry to be seen. Hungry to be chosen. Hungry to be held, mirrored, rescued, validated.

In conscious relating, neither person arrives starving.

There is desire, yes—but not desperation. There is attraction—but not collapse. There is openness—but not self-erasure.

Conscious relating begins when two people can hold themselves.

Not perfectly. Not rigidly. But reliably.

A conscious partner does not feed on your wounds, your mystery, your erotic charge, or your spiritual language. They are not intoxicated by your intensity, nor threatened by your depth. They do not rush to define, possess, or consume.

They meet you without needing you to regulate them.

Conscious relating is alignment, not excitement. Chemistry happens in the body. Connection happens in the nervous system. But conscious relating happens at the level of values.

This is where many modern relationships fail—because alignment is mistaken for attraction.

Alignment means:

- How you treat power
- How you handle conflict
- How you relate to money, time, work, rest
- How you hold responsibility
- How do you repair harm
- How you speak when you are frustrated
- How you behave when no one is watching

These are not sexy questions.

But they are the questions that determine whether love can last without distortion.

Conscious relating is the meeting of:

- Emotional values (how feelings are held and repaired)
- Mental values (how meaning is made and truth is handled)
- Physical values (how bodies are respected, paced, and protected)
- Spiritual values (how power, devotion, and transcendence are held without bypass)

When these are aligned, intimacy feels clean. Not intoxicating. Not overwhelming. Clean.

The soul does not rush

One of the great lies of modern spirituality is that recognition must be instant.

"You'll know immediately."

"When it's right, it's effortless."

"The soul remembers."

Sometimes the soul remembers trauma. That intensity you feel is not soul recognition but trauma and wound recognition.

Conscious relating unfolds slowly, not because there is a lack of desire, but because there is respect for reality. Time is allowed to reveal character. Nervous systems are allowed to settle. Fantasies are allowed to dissolve.

A conscious partner is not afraid of time. They are not in a hurry to lock you in, define you, or access your body. They understand that intimacy without integration creates harm.

Conscious relating requires inner strength, not attraction techniques

You do not "manifest" conscious relating by visualising harder.

You become available to it by strengthening yourself. You become sovereign first and realise your own self-worth.

This is the part that is often skipped—because it is not glamorous.

To be ready for conscious relating, you must strengthen:

- Your emotional capacity to feel without flooding
- Your somatic capacity to sense safety and danger accurately
- Your mental clarity to distinguish pattern from promise
- Your spiritual integrity to recognise humility versus performance

This means doing the unromantic work:

- Healing the inner child so they are not running the show
- Integrating the inner teenager so rebellion does not masquerade as desire
- Embodying the sovereign adult so decisions come from steadiness, not longing

Only then does attraction change.

Not because you are trying to attract differently, but because misalignment no longer feels tolerable.

Conscious relating does not chase.

In unconscious dynamics, people chase recognition.

In conscious relating, recognition is mutual.

There is no audition. No proving. No spiritual seduction.

Both people feel free and choose to stay.

This is the paradox: when you stop chasing connection, you become capable of receiving it.

Not because you are detached. But because you are rooted.

What conscious relating feels like (experientially)

It feels like:

- Calm interest rather than urgency
- Curiosity without intrusion
- Desire that does not override discernment
- Presence that does not need performance
- Boundaries that do not rupture intimacy

It feels like your body is relaxing over time, not bracing. It feels like conversations that deepen rather than destabilise. It feels like a disagreement that does not threaten the connection. It feels like your life is expanding—not shrinking—to make room for love.

The quiet truth

Conscious relating is not rare because people are broken. It is rare because it requires maturity on all levels at once.

Most people are developed in one or two dimensions—and underdeveloped in the others.

But when emotional, mental, physical, and spiritual integrity align within you, something changes.

You stop asking:

"Do they want me?"

And start asking:

"Does this feel aligned with who I am becoming?"

From that place, love is no longer something you chase or fear losing.

It becomes something you recognise.

Quietly. Clearly. Without confusion.

And that is conscious relating.

The New Paradigm of Conscious Relating

We are moving away from the traditional constructs of marriage. And here is why- it is extremely difficult to cohesively merge two different lifestyles, family systems, and values. What works better is space- having your own individual lives while enjoying the company of each other. Yes, commitment is present. But it is a choice, not one made out of force or societal pressures. This type of a dynamic does many things- it makes you cherish and value each other; and it creates that extra effort factor which dies away when you cohabitate. Ultimately most marriages lose their spark not because there is something evidently wrong with the couple but because they are now in a rut living like roommates.

I call this type of a new paradigm- a soul marriage. Where you are connected and separate as well. A separate-togetherness. Where, every day you choose each other not because you have to but because you want to. And above all, in this union neither one loses themselves.

To the Masculine and the Feminine—A Message.

Each one of us carries both energies: the feminine, the sacred receiver, the creatrix who holds the womb codes of creation itself; and the masculine, the provider, the grounding, the initiator who builds, protects, and directs. Today, the world is imbalanced—not because women have changed, but because women have been forced to become hyper-masculine, overextending themselves, doing everything, holding everything, because too many men have abandoned the throne of their own sacred masculinity. So, this is my message to the masculine: Rise. Rise to meet your match not only in coin, but in heart, in integrity, in spirit. Hold the feminine in truth. Don't run when the road gets rocky. Don't vanish once your needs are met. Recognise a woman of worth and meet her there—fully, consistently, courageously. And to the feminine: Raise your standards. Stop romanticising potential. When your intuition whispers its first warning, when a red flag flickers like a candle in the wind, don't silence it. Don't rationalise it. Every time I suffered, it was because I betrayed my own knowing. Self-reliance is not hyper-independence; it is the journey back to your wholeness. Masculine or feminine—your work is the same: grow up, rise, and love from a place of truth, not survival. Only then can we meet each other as equals, as sovereigns, as the fullest expressions of who we were always meant to be.

Activation: The Moment the Feminine Rises

Your most obvious question to me may be: "Why didn't you wake up after your abusive marriage? Why did you endure the endless masks of manipulation, the distortions, the darkness of the masculine?"

And here is my truth.

I was not resting in my sovereignty yet.

I was blinded by the myth of the "twin flame," by the idea that salvation would come in the shape of a man. I was convinced that safety came from masculine arms, not from my own spine. I believed grounding meant leaning on someone else, not rooting myself in my own being. I thought I would not survive without a man's love—until the day I rose and realised I was the one I was waiting for.

And secondly, these experiences were my initiation.

I walked through fire after fire, betrayal after betrayal, illusion after illusion—not because I was weak, but because I was being forged. Broken open in a thousand ways so I could rise in one. My wounds became my wisdom; my suffering became my medicine. I walked through the shadows so I could speak for the women who have been silenced, for the ones who could not rise, for the ones still trapped in the dark.

I speak not just for myself—I speak in unison with the sacred feminine across lifetimes.

And this is the activation: Enough. Enough of shrinking. Enough of tolerating pain because we are strong. Enough of accepting crumbs because we once thought we were starving. Enough of mistaking chaos for passion, manipulation for love, control for protection.

We, the feminine, are not here to be tested again and again. We are not here to endure atrocity after atrocity. We are not here to be the emotional dumping grounds of unhealed men.

Our ability to tolerate pain does not mean pain is our home.

We are the temple. We are the throne. We are the fire. We are the medicine.

And now we rise with clarity, not confusion. With discernment, not desperation. With sovereignty, not longing.

From this moment forward, hear this as a command from the sacred feminine:

"Treat us as sacred—or step aside." Match our truth—or fall away. Rise in integrity—or lose access.

We are not waiting anymore. We are choosing ourselves.

This is the reclamation. This is the phoenix moment. This is the line in the sand. The feminine returns to her throne—and the world must learn to meet her there.

A Message to You, Dear Reader- "The Rebalancing of the Sacred"

> *"The yin and the yang are opposite forces, yet it is the combination of these two that makes the world complete."*
>
> **– Lao Tzu**

If at any point in this book you feel that I am "male-bashing," let me tell you this directly: that is not my intention, nor is it my truth. I am not here to demonise masculinity; I am here to illuminate the patterns that harm both men and women. I share these stories not to divide, but to awaken. For most of human history, the feminine was considered sacred — the axis of life, intuition, creation, and divine intelligence. Patriarchy is a relatively recent interruption, born when society believed that controlling the wild woman was necessary for survival. As we stand at the threshold of a new era — one where these old structures are dissolving — we are being called into balance again.

The masculine is stronger when he can own his vulnerability, and the feminine is more powerful when she stands in her sovereignty, honoured at the centre of the sacred, where she has always belonged. True healing demands that both rise. Presence must replace performance. Respect must replace dominance. And connection must replace fear. This book is not a battle cry against men — it is an invitation for all of us to evolve.

The message is clear, and it can no longer be whispered: the feminine must rise in her sovereignty, or she will continue to be diminished by a world that profits from her self-annihilation. As long as she remains in the paradigm of self-sacrifice, self-abandonment, and emotional contortion, she will be drained, distorted, and devoured by systems built on her silence. The feminine must become more discerning, more self-serving in the healthiest sense — loyal to her own truth, devoted to her intuition, anchored in her worth.

And the masculine, too, stands at a crossroads. If he continues to bypass his inner world, if he refuses to face the grief, fear, and tenderness buried beneath his armour, he will remain entangled in ego, domination, and emotional paralysis. His refusal to look inward will not only wound others — it will devour him from within.

So let this be understood: this is not a battle cry; it is a warning. Harmony cannot be restored through denial. Union cannot be reborn through avoidance. The sacred balance — the divine dance between feminine and masculine — can only return when both energies are willing to evolve.

The feminine must reclaim herself.

The masculine must confront himself.

And together, they must rise — not in hierarchy, but in harmony. This is the revival of sacred balance. This is the call of our time. And this is where the new world begins.

Where We Are Headed: The Next Evolution of Relationship

The future of a relationship is not dominance vs submission.

It is wholeness meeting wholeness.

It is women becoming:

- Self-reliant
- Nervous-system regulated
- Energetically sovereign
- Anchored in self-worth

And men being invited—not forced—into:

- Their heart space
- Emotional literacy
- Felt experience
- Vulnerability without shame

Men do not open their hearts through lectures, ultimatums, or intellectualisation.

They open their hearts by feeling. Feeling grief. Feeling love. Feeling fear. Feeling tenderness.

This requires exiting the head and allowing Shakti—emotion, instinct, life force—to move freely.

And it requires women who can:

- Hold their own ground
- Create safe containers
- Lead without controlling
- Trust without collapsing

This is where Shiva and Shakti align—within both men and women.

Not two wounded children throwing tantrums for love and attention,

but two integrated beings choosing each other consciously.

CHAPTER 14

REWRITING LOVE FROM THE INSIDE OUT

I am not a relationship expert because I studied attachment theory in isolation.

I am a relational expert because I lived the patterns, survived the traps, metabolised the harm, and emerged with clarity instead of cynicism.

I have walked through longing, fantasy, spiritual bypass, emotional manipulation, over-giving, erotic confusion, and the collapse that follows when women abandon themselves in the name of love. I have felt what it is like to be chosen and discarded, idealised and reduced, desired and dehumanised.

And then—I did the harder work.

I stopped outsourcing safety. I stopped seeking validation. I stopped confusing intensity with connection.

What I recycled was not trauma for sympathy—but wisdom for sovereignty.

This work is not about helping women "get a man."

It is about helping women come home to themselves—so that whether they remain single or attract a partner of equal calibre, they are no longer negotiating their worth.

The Core Realisation That Changed Everything

I did not need a man to ground my intensity. I needed to become grounded enough to hold it myself.

What I had mistaken for restlessness was high life-force energy without containment. What I had mistaken for chemistry was nervous-system activation without safety.

The truth was confronting and liberating:

I had to invoke Shiva within myself.

Stillness. Containment. Presence.

Witness consciousness.

Not as a concept.

As a felt, lived nervous-system state.

When I stopped searching for a man to anchor me, regulate me, or stabilise me, something radical happened:

I became safe inside my own body.

From that place, desire transformed.

Love recalibrated. My standards stopped being defensive and became non-negotiable. I was no longer asking love to rescue me from myself. I was meeting love as someone already home.

From Over-Giving to Self-Referencing

I stepped out of the caretaker role.

Not because I became cold— but because I became full.

I rewired the belief that love requires self-erasure. I stopped being the emotional regulator for men who had not met their own hearts. I stopped mistaking potential for presence. My nourishment began to flow to me first—

I became the empress of my own garden first and then to those I consciously chose to love. This is not selfishness. This is energetic literacy. A woman who feeds herself emotionally is no longer harvestable by predators, unavailable men, or spiritualized manipulators.

The Sun Principle: I Do Not Revolve Around a Man

In my new paradigm, I am not the moon to a man's orbit.

I am the sun. I have my own rhythm. My own gravity. My own creative force.

If a partner enters my life, he does not become my axis. He becomes a co-creator, not a centre.

I will not lose my identity in partnership. I will not shrink my passions to make love comfortable. I will not abandon my inner alignment for relational security.

And paradoxically, this is the only place from which true partnership becomes possible.

Loneliness, the Divine, and the End of the Searching Frequency

One of the greatest myths sold to women is that being alone is a problem to be solved.

Loneliness, when untreated, drives:

- Over-attachment
- Fantasy bonding
- Settling
- Emotional bargaining

But what changed everything for me was this: I stopped trying to fill loneliness with people. I already knew how to be in my own company. I could sit alone in cafés. Travel alone. Create alone. Be silent without panic.

And more importantly, I felt the Divine with me. My relationship and communication with the Divine became stronger. My intuition sharpened. I felt alive. Not as dogma. Not as performance. But as presence. When I cultivated an internal relationship with something larger than romantic validation, loneliness stopped feeling like an absence. It became space.

Space to breathe. Space to listen. Space to discern.

I no longer broadcast the searching frequency.

That frequency—the subtle energetic hum of "please choose me"—is what predators, avoidant men, and emotionally unavailable partners respond to.

Containment ended the broadcast. I was no longer scanning the world for completion.

I was inhabiting myself.

Why This Makes Me a Relational Expert

Because I am not selling fantasy. I am teaching integration. Because I do not promise romance. I promise self-respect. Because I am not helping women chase love. I am helping them become unavailable to anything misaligned.

My authority comes from embodiment, not ideology.

How I Took Charge of Myself

My first hunger for partnership did not come from romance. It came from fear. Not the dramatic kind. Not panic.

But the slow, corrosive understanding that as a woman moving through the world alone, I was not safe. I was objectified on solo trips. Hunted in therapy spaces that were meant to be containers of care. Propositioned inside my own healing practice—by men who mistook my presence, my empathy, or my attention for sexual availability.

It happened often enough that a belief took root, quietly and convincingly: As a woman, I am not safe in the world on my own. So, partnership began to feel less like desire and more like insurance- a necessity for life itself. A shield.

A body beside mine that might deter intrusion.

This is not a belief many women admit to. But many live by it.

Step One: Securing Safety Without Apology

The first thing I had to do was take charge of safety—not symbolically, not spiritually, but practically. No affirmations. No mantras. No bypass.

I moved in with my Shih Tzu.

That decision alone changed everything. Animals do not gaslight your instincts. They do not minimise the threat. They respond to energy honestly.

My dog became both my companion and sentinel. He anchored my inner child in the body and the present moment. He also made me visible in the world in a way that felt grounded, not exposed.

I hired full-time help.

This is a detail people often romanticise away, but it mattered. Knowing there was another human presence—reliable, routine, predictable—shifted my nervous system out of constant vigilance.

I chose a building with biometric security.

Key cards. Cameras. Guards. Systems.

It is sometimes shocking the lengths women must go to secure what should be a basic human right: safety. But once I stopped resenting that truth and simply responded to it, my body finally began to rest.

Safety is not a luxury. It is the foundation of sovereignty.

Step Two: Choosing the Right Terrain

I learned something essential about myself: I could not survive in nature alone. And I could not survive in the relentless intensity of city life either. I needed both.

So, I chose a place where trees and traffic coexisted. Where birdsong didn't require isolation, and civilisation didn't require hyper-vigilance. A place where I could step into green space and still order groceries without a logistical operation.

This balance was not aesthetic. It was neurological.

My system began to recalibrate. I slept better. My digestion changed. My breath deepened.

Healing does not happen in environments that constantly contradict your nervous system.

Step Three: Rhythm as Medicine

Once safety and terrain were in place, something unexpected happened.

My rhythms started to heal. Not dramatically. Not all at once.

Quietly.

I began investing in the mundane acts that no one posts about.

Cooking. Cleaning. Caring for plants. Walking my dog at the same time each day. These were not chores. They were regulation rituals.

The consistency of tending to life—food, floors, fur, foliage—stitched me back into my body. My inner child, who had lived in hyper-alertness for years, finally began to soften.

My dog, being the keeper of my inner child, mirrored my own grounding right back to me- he was happier and calmer. Animals mirror what words cannot. He responded not to my narrative, but to my state. Care became circular rather than performative.

Step Four: Choosing Soul-Fuelling Work

I stopped doing work that merely paid me. I started doing work that fed me.

It meant choosing engagements where my intelligence, ethics, and sensitivity were valued—not exploited. Work became a place of contribution, not depletion. And something surprising happened: As my work aligned with my values, my tolerance for nonsense dropped. I no longer had the energy to entertain dynamics that drained me emotionally or intellectually. My time became precious—not because I was busy, but because I was present.

Step Five: Disengaging from Noise

At some point, I disengaged from politics, gossip, and emotional drama—not because I didn't care, but because my nervous system had been on fire for too long.

I realised that outrage addiction is just another form of dysregulation. So, I opted out. I stopped consuming content designed to provoke rather than inform. I stopped participating in conversations that revolved around blame, speculation, or moral performance. And in the silence that followed, something remarkable occurred: My logic sharpened alongside my intuition. Not instead of it. With it.

This was important. For years, intuition had been romanticised as the antidote to logic, and logic had been used to override intuition. I learned they are meant to work together. Logis is just the other side of the coin that is intuition.

Discernment lives in that marriage.

Step Six: Relating as Choice, Not Obligation

I began engaging with people only when it felt good. This sounds selfish until you try it. I stopped forcing the connection. Stopped staying polite out of habit. Stopped overriding discomfort to preserve harmony.

And the moment a dynamic became draining—emotionally, energetically, conversationally—I disengaged.

No speeches. No explanations. No guilt. Just withdrawal of access. This was not avoidance. It was discernment.

The result was immediate and unmistakable: fewer people, better quality. Less stimulation, more depth. Silence that felt like relief rather than loneliness.

What Changed fundamentally?

When I look back, I see that I did not become "stronger" in the performative sense. I did not harden. I did not armour myself with ideology or bravado.

I structured my life so my nervous system could finally stand down.

That changed everything. My need for partnership shifted—not because I became anti-love, but because I no longer needed a man to act as a buffer between me and the world. I was no longer seeking protection through proximity. I had taken charge of myself.

Step Seven: Healing the Father Wound

I worked on healing my father wound actively. I became sovereign, took charge of my life-yes, but I also softened towards my father. I started sharing my emotional vulnerabilities with him. I brought back the closeness we once shared- when I was a child and he would show me the wildness of nature. And in turn, my father softened as well. He started relying on me emotionally and energetically. I became the backbone for his decisions. The universe nudged me to not only stand in my power but to heal the wounding at its source. And I no longer needed an inadequate man to validate me ever again because the work was not just emotional it was soul-deep.

The Quiet Power of Self-Command

Taking charge did not make me less open. It made me more precise.

It did not make me cold. It made me clear.

I stopped confusing exposure with bravery and endurance with strength. I stopped believing that being "spiritual" meant being endlessly available.

Instead, I learned something radical:

Safety, rhythm, clarity, and self-respect are not barriers to love.

They are prerequisites for it. Once those were in place, something softened. Not because the world became safer—but because I had stopped outsourcing my safety to hope, partnership, or luck.

I had built it.

And from that place, I could finally choose. Not out of fear. Not out of hunger. But out of alignment.

25 Principles for Attracting the Aligned Partner

This section is not about manifesting love. It is about attracting alignment.

Aligned partnership does not arrive because you want it badly enough, work on yourself hard enough, or visualise clearly enough. It arrives when your internal systems—emotional, somatic, psychological, and spiritual—are in sync.

Love does not enter chaos willingly. It recognises structure.

What follows is not advice. It is a record of embodied truths that emerged only after patterns were seen clearly, wounds were taken responsibility for, self-abandonment stopped being romanticised, love and self-worth stopped being outsourced.

1. Safety Is the First Language of Love

Before desire can deepen, the nervous system must exhale.

Many women are taught to prioritise chemistry, attraction, and intensity. Safety is framed as optional, boring, or something to be negotiated later. But the body does not open to intensity—it tenses. Desire may ignite, but intimacy cannot root without safety.

For years, I overrode this knowing. I allowed men access to my time, body, and emotional world because they were charming, wounded, spiritually articulate, or magnetically drawn to my energy. My shoulders tightened. My breath shortened. My intuition whispered. My body rang alarm bells. It shook with a hard NO. And still, I stayed and gave in.

Until I reached the final refuge of self-abandonment.

The shift came when safety became non-negotiable. Not a hope. Not a preference. A filter.

I said no to male friends who lingered too long in innuendo, to potential partners who commented on my body before my mind, to dynamics that felt consuming rather than steady. Even when attraction was present, I honoured my deeper need to feel protected rather than pursued.

I created a sanctuary of self—my home, my time, my nervous system—where ambiguous or objectifying energy simply could not enter.

Strategy for attraction:

When safety becomes your baseline, unsafe men self-eliminate. Aligned men approach slowly, respectfully, and with consistency. They do not test your boundaries; they recognise them.

2. Stillness Is Not Absence — It Is Authority

For a long time, I believed I needed a man who could hold my intensity.

My Shakti was fierce—creative, sexual, emotional, spiritual. What I did not recognise was that I was outsourcing containment. I was asking men to regulate energy, I had not yet learned to hold myself.

This is where many women get trapped: mistaking the ability to be "held" by another for maturity, when in fact it is often a sign of unintegrated power.

The turning point came when I stopped searching for Shiva outside of me and began cultivating him within.

Through daily nervous-system regulation—ritual, silence, nature, rhythm, presence—stillness stopped being something I longed for and became something I lived inside. Stillness ceased to mean emptiness. It became an authority.

A woman who can hold her own energy does not leak urgency. She does not require someone else to stabilise her. She herself is the stillness she is seeking for. She is not a beacon of restless search anymore.

Strategy for attraction:

Men who lack presence feel exposed around grounded women. Men with integrated masculine energy feel drawn—not to dominate—but to co-create calm.

3. Healing the Inner Child Without Romantic Substitution

Unhealed inner children do not seek love. They seek regulation. They seek holding, they seek nurture.

When the inner child remains unmet, romantic relationships become the stage upon which unmet needs play out: soothing, reassurance, protection, mirroring, rescue. This is not intimacy; it is substitution.

Through deep re-parenting, I created a home where my inner child could exist without performance. This healing went beyond just therapy. I started creating an actual safe haven for my inner child. She could sing, wander, rest, cry, and play without being impressive or pleasing. I listened to her fears. I protected her rhythms. I became the best mother to her.

When she stopped reaching outward for soothing, my attraction to emotionally unavailable men collapsed almost overnight.

Strategy for attraction:

When your inner child is held by you, you stop bonding through wounds. You attract men who meet you as a woman—not as a project, patient, or fantasy.

4. Integrating the Inner Teenager

The inner teenager carries desire, rebellion, sexuality, anger, and identity.

Unintegrated, she seeks intensity, validation, and recognition through others. Integrated, she becomes discerning, confident, and expressive. The unhealed inner teenager is the one driving all your one-night stands and situationships.

I stopped outsourcing rebellion through relationships—through risky dynamics, unavailable men, or emotional drama—and started honouring her directly. Creativity, truth-telling, clear boundaries, and embodied pleasure gave her a voice.

Strategy:

Men attracted to chaos disengage. Men attracted to confidence stay curious.

5. The Sovereign Adult as the Primary Decision-Maker

Sovereignty begins when the adult self leads. Not the wounded child. Not the romantic idealist. Not the rescuer.

When decisions came from my grounded adult self—pace, boundaries, timing—attraction shifted fundamentally. Drama no longer entered easily. Confusion stopped feeling seductive.

Strategy:

You attract what your decision-maker is, not what your heart hopes for.

6. Freedom Is Rhythm, Not Rebellion

Freedom is not constant movement or defiance. It is rhythm.

My nervous system thrives on cadence—how I wake, cook, clean, walk, write, work, and rest. These are not lifestyle quirks; they are regulation mechanisms. I stopped bending my life around potential partners. My rhythm became sacred. Anyone who disrupted it—emotionally, energetically, logistically—was incompatible.

This was not rigidity. It was self-trust.

Strategy:

Aligned partners respect rhythm. Misaligned ones disrupt it.

7. Standards Are Self-Respect in Motion

Standards are not demands placed on others. They are filters that protect your life force.

I stopped justifying my standards and started living them. Relationships that drained me were exited cleanly, without explanation or drama.

The rule became simple: If it costs my peace, it costs too much.

Strategy:

High-quality partners are relieved by standards. Low-quality ones feel exposed.

8. Emotional Literacy Over Emotional Intensity

Intensity is cheap. Literacy is rare.

I stopped being impressed by emotional overflow and started valuing emotional precision—men who could name feelings, track patterns, repair ruptures, and stay accountable without collapsing into shame or defensiveness.

Strategy:

Model clarity. Men incapable of it will feel inadequate and exit.

9. Repair Is the Real Measure of Love

Anyone can connect during harmony. Few can repair during rupture.

I began watching how conflict was handled—not avoided, not escalated, but repaired. Did the other person listen? Reflect? Take responsibility? Change behaviour? Or were they just avoidant or even aggressive?

Strategy:

If repair is absent, intimacy is too.

10. Erotic Sovereignty (Not Availability)

Desire without self-possession invites misuse.

When I stopped leaking erotic energy for connection and rooted it within my own body, my sexuality became calm, potent, and self-directed. I was no longer available. I was selectively receptive.

Strategy:

Men who rely on conquest lose interest. Men who value depth lean in.

11. Solitude as Skill, Not Punishment

I learned to live well alone. Not waiting. Not longing.

Simply inhabiting my life fully. Solitude stopped feeling like absence and became a sign of emotional maturity and fullness.

Strategy:

Men afraid of intimacy avoid women at home in themselves. Men ready for partnership recognise solitude as stability.

12. Discernment Without Cynicism. Meeting the Person not the Potential

Discernment is calm. It takes time to learn the person and discern their true nature. Potential does not equal reality.

I learned to read patterns without demonising men or romanticising potential. A lot of women, myself included, are guilty of this- we project our "the one" fantasies on week 1 of knowing the guy. And we are grossly disappointed at yet another failed connection when the man simply does not meet our expectations or worse yet ghosts us. I repeat- potential DOES

NOT equal reality. Take time to unravel the person. Red flags must be noted, not debated. Green flags need to be observed over time.

Strategy:

Clarity attracts consistency. Urgency feeds chaos. Allow reality and actions to match the perceived potential before falling for "the one."

13. Financial & Energetic Self-Stability

Dependence—emotional or financial—distorts attraction.

I stabilised my life systems so love became a choice, not a strategy. When survival is no longer on the line, discernment sharpens.

Strategy:

Men seeking power leave. Men seeking partnership arrive.

14. Integrity Between Words and Actions

I stopped listening to explanations and started watching behaviour. Consistency became the loudest signal. Promises lost their power. Reality spoke.

Strategy:

You do not reward potential. You respond to the pattern. You see their actions- over time.

15. Allowing Love to Be Slow

Fast bonds are trauma bonds. Filter, filter, filter- this is not being picky, it is setting high standards. Ask the hard questions- get to know their intentions- get to know them before allowing access. Allow time to reveal their true nature and character. Most men do not play the long game in this world of instant gratification.

I learned to let attraction unfold without acceleration. Safety deepened before intimacy did.

Strategy:

Aligned partners deepen their connection instead of rushing it.

16. Curiosity Over Projection

I stopped projecting who someone could be and became curious about who they were. I stopped falling for the potential of the man; I became real about where he was in that moment. I asked real and hard questions early on. That itself acts as a great filter.

Strategy:

Projection attracts fantasy. Curiosity attracts truth.

17. Mutuality as Baseline

I stopped over-giving to earn love. Reciprocity became the minimum requirement.

Strategy:

Love is mutual, or it is management.

18. Calm Is Not Boring

Many of us were conditioned to associate chaos with aliveness.

Calm initially felt unfamiliar—until it felt like home.

Strategy:

When calm feels safe, alignment becomes visible.

19. Boundaries Without Drama

I learned to say no without explanation- and I watched for the response. If met with anything but respect, I exit.

Strategy:

Drama attracts dysregulation. Calm boundaries attract respect.

20. Embodiment Over Performance

I stopped performing femininity and started inhabiting my body.

Strategy:

Embodiment attracts presence. Performance attracts consumption.

21. Shared Values Over Shared Trauma

Bonding over wounds creates loops. Sharing too much too soon is another sign that wounds are colliding.

Bonding over values creates futures.

Strategy:

Reach a stage of wholeness first and share from there rather than trauma bonding over past wounding.

22. Time as the Great Revealer. Effort matters.

I let time do the work. I watched for effort even in the small things.

Strategy:

What is real deepens. What is false dissolves. Because true love is not an illusory facade that crumbles or vanishes. True love stands the test of time.

23. Listening to the Body First

I learned to trust sensation over story. I now trust my own intuition like a radar, as soon as there is an internal alarm- even the first one- I heed.

Strategy:

Listen to your intuition- we all have it. Your mind can rationalize but your body knows the truth.

24. Wholeness Before Union

Your ultimate partner is not your missing half. They are your physical, emotional, mental, and spiritual counterpart.

This level of partnership requires integration of the:

- Inner child

- Inner teenager
- Sovereign adult

Only wholeness recognises wholeness.

Strategy:

Integrative work is key. Integration of all the parts of us that are running the show.

25. You Attract What You Are Ready to Hold

Aligned love does not arrive because you want it.

It arrives because you are structured to receive it.

Strategy:

Prepare your container for the one you want to walk beside in a way that even when you are by yourself, you are complete.

This is not self-improvement. It is self-return.

And from that place, love no longer feels like a gamble.

It feels like recognition. You simply do not attract misalignment; you arrive within yourself- a place from which alignment meets you.

Somatic & Intuitive Indicators of an Aligned Partnership

(This is meant to feel visceral, honest, and unmistakable. No romance. No theory. Just the truth your body already knows.)

This is not a checklist for perfection. It is a body-based truth test. If you find yourself explaining away what your body feels, pause.

The body does not speak in paragraphs. It speaks in sensation.

1. **Your breath drops lower in your body**

   Not during attraction—but after time passes. Your shoulders soften. Your belly moves when you breathe. You are not holding yourself together.

   If not: shallow breath, tight chest, constant alertness.

   Alignment feels like exhaling.

2. **You do not feel watched**

   You are not monitoring your tone, words, clothes, or reactions. You can be quiet without being asked what's wrong. You can change your mind without consequences.

   If not: hyper-awareness, self-editing, subtle fear.

   Safety is the absence of surveillance.

3. **Desire does not hijack your judgment**

   You want them, but you do not lose yourself. You can still say no. You can still pause. You do not feel pulled past your own edge.

   If not: urgency, collapse, bargaining with your intuition.

   Real desire coexists with choice.

4. **Your body does not freeze during intimacy**

   You stay present. No dissociation. No going numb. No need to "get through it."

   If not: bracing, leaving your body, performing.

   The body knows when it is safe to stay.

5. **After seeing them, you feel clearer—not scrambled**

   Your thoughts settle. You don't replay conversations trying to decode meaning. You don't feel emotionally hungover.

   If not: rumination, confusion, anxiety.

Confusion is not depth. It is disorientation.

6. **You do not feel pressure to be exceptional**

   You don't have to be:

   - Sexy
   - Spiritual
   - Interesting
   - Healed

   You can just exist.

   If not: performing femininity, wisdom, or strength.

   Love that requires performance is extraction.

7. **Your gut does not tighten when you express a need**

   You say what you need—and your body does not brace for backlash. No pre-emptive apology. No rehearsing.

   If not: stomach clench, throat lock, heart race.

   Needs are not negotiations in safe love.

8. **Conflict does not trigger survival mode**

   Your body stays present. You don't freeze, fawn, fight, or disappear. You don't feel smaller afterwards.

   If not: collapse, shutdown, self-blame.

   Repair should calm the body, not cost it.

9. **Your inner child relaxes instead of reaching**

   You don't feel like a little girl trying to be chosen. You are not waiting for reassurance. You are not scanning for abandonment.

   If not: longing, clinging, fear of loss.

   When the inner child is calm, the bond is clean.

10. **Your body does not flinch at the future**

    When you imagine tomorrow, next month, next year—

    There is no tightening. No dread. No pressure.

If not: heaviness, anxiety, "something feels off."
The body senses trajectory before the mind names it.

11. **You feel more solid in yourself, not diluted**
    You don't feel spread thin. Your boundaries stay intact. Your energy does not leak.
    If not: exhaustion, emotional depletion, numbness.
    Love should fortify you.
12. **You don't feel compelled to explain yourself**
    You are understood enough. You are not constantly clarifying, justifying, or translating your inner world.
    If not: over-explaining, frustration, invisibility.
    Being seen feels simple.
13. **Your sexuality feels grounded, not performative**
    Desire feels steady—not frantic. You are in your body, not offering it. You feel sovereign in pleasure.
    If not: disconnection, pressure, erotic leaking, even dissociation.
    True intimacy leaves you fuller.
14. **You do not abandon your life to maintain closeness**
    Your routines stay intact. Your friendships, work, solitude, and rhythm remain yours.
    If not: shrinking world, prioritising them over yourself.
    Alignment does not require disappearance.
15. **Your body says, "This is sustainable"**
    Not exciting. Not dramatic.
    Sustainable.
    Your system recognises:
    "I can live inside this."
    If not: cycles, highs and crashes, instability.

The body recognises home before the mind trusts it.

The Final Body Truth

Ask yourself one question—without thinking:

"Do I feel more alive here—or more on guard?"

That answer is enough.

Aligned partnership does not electrify your wounds. It does not awaken survival. It allows the body to stand down. And when the body is no longer bracing, love stops feeling like a risk and starts feeling like recognition. That is the signal.

Toward Wholeness: How Men Can Meet the Empowered Woman

This book does not demonise men.

What it does is shine a steady, uncompromising light on the shadow patterns of unhealed relating.

The traps described in these pages are not born from cruelty alone. They are born from conditioning, emotional neglect, and a deep rupture from the heart. When we strip the behaviours down to their core, what remains is not a villain, but a wounded human being who never learned how to feel safe.

Over years of lived experience, observation, and reflection, one truth has revealed itself again and again: many of the relational patterns that harm women today originate from men never being permitted to be vulnerable.

My own father was once a soft, creative boy. Sensitive. Curious. Alive. But the world did not nurture that softness—it demanded armour. To survive, he hardened. To function, he learned restraint. To be accepted, he hid. This story is not unique. It is generational. Men are taught early to "toughen up," to suppress emotion, to translate pain into performance, silence, or dominance. Tears are shamed. Fear is mocked. Tenderness is feminised and therefore rejected.

And when the heart is exiled, it does not disappear—it finds distorted ways to be fed.

This is where many modern relational traps emerge. Emotional intimacy becomes a strategy rather than a state of being. Connection becomes transactional. Vulnerability is performed, not embodied. Men learn to simulate closeness to meet their needs—sexual, emotional, or egoic—without ever truly opening themselves to the risk of being seen.

The tragedy is this: the deeper longing underneath these patterns is genuine. The hunger for love is real. But without access to the heart, love becomes a game.

Even the pathological liar. Even the emotionally unavailable man. Even the narcissist.

At the core of these patterns often lives a profoundly unhealed child—frequently one who never received attuned nurturing, safety, or emotional mirroring. This does not excuse harm. But it does explain it.

And explanation matters, because without it we remain trapped in cycles of blame, polarisation, and hopelessness.

It is important to be very clear here: it is not the job of women to heal men.

Women are not rehabilitation centres for wounded masculinity. Love is not therapy. Intimacy is not a replacement for accountability. No amount of patience, understanding, or self-sacrifice can transform a man who is unwilling to face himself.

Healing begins only when a man does two essential things:

A. Takes accountability
B. Accepts help

Accountability means owning patterns without justification or defensiveness. It means recognising harm. It means saying, "This is mine to work with."

Accepting help means allowing guidance, mentorship, therapy, community, and reflection. It means relinquishing the illusion of self-sufficiency. It means understanding that strength is not the absence of vulnerability—it is the capacity to stay present with it.

Healing takes work. Real work. Often uncomfortable work.

So how can a man arrive at a place of wholeness where he can truly meet an empowered woman?

The indicators are not perfect. They are marked by presence.

Is he willing to grow, even when it destabilises his self-image?

Is he open, or does he become defensive when challenged?

Can he be vulnerable without collapsing into shame or control?

Is he able to sit with discomfort rather than manipulate his way out of it?

These are the markers of a man who is doing the work.

And when such a man begins to open—when he steps out of performance and into truth—something else is required.

Women must give space for vulnerability without control. This does not mean tolerating abuse. It does not mean minimising boundaries. It does not mean shrinking needs or desires. It means not weaponising a man's openness. Not managing his emotions. Not scripting his healing.

An empowered woman does not dominate vulnerability—she witnesses it.

She holds her ground while allowing his process. She honours his masculinity without policing it. She does not mother him back to wholeness, but she also does not punish him for being human.

This is where true relating is born—not from dominance or submission, but from mutual responsibility.

The healed man does not fear the empowered woman. He is not intimidated by her clarity, her boundaries, or her strength. He does not need to trap her, control her, or diminish her to feel whole.

He meets her—not from armour, but from heart.

And the empowered woman does not need to rescue or reform him. She chooses him because he is already choosing himself.

This is the deeper invitation behind Man Traps.

Not to harden women against men. Not to shame men into silence.

But to call both into truth.

When men return to the heart, and women return to themselves, relationships stop being battlegrounds—and start becoming places of shared becoming.

That is not idealism.

That is the work.

The Quiet Throne: Where Intuition Becomes Law and the Heart Is Finally Honoured

There comes a moment in every life when the noise falls away.

Not because the world has grown quieter—but because you have learned which voices no longer deserve authority. The opinions. The projections. The expectations. The inherited scripts about love, sacrifice, patience, and endurance. At some point, you stop asking for permission to know what you know.

This is that moment.

If this book has done its work, you are no longer searching for answers outside yourself. You are listening inward—not anxiously, not desperately, but with a steady, grounded reverence for the intelligence that has always lived in your body, your breath, your bones.

Your intuition was never broken.

It was overridden. Overridden by a culture that told you to doubt yourself. By relationships that rewarded self-betrayal. By stale narratives that glorified suffering. By love stories that confused chaos with destiny.

But intuition does not shout. It waits.

It waits patiently while you test every other authority. It watches while you rationalise red flags, reinterpret discomfort, override sensation, and call endurance "strength." And when you are finally exhausted—when the mind runs out of excuses, and the heart can no longer tolerate betrayal—intuition rises, not as drama, but as clarity.

It feels like this: A quiet no. A grounded yes. A deep exhale. A sense of coming home.

This is the throne you were always meant to sit on.

Not a throne of domination. Not a throne of superiority. But a throne of self-trust.

From this place, everything changes.

You stop asking, "Will I be chosen?"

And start asking, "Is this aligned with my truth?"

You stop bending to be lovable. You stop shrinking to be safe. You stop performing healing, femininity, spirituality, or strength. You simply become real. And reality has its own gravity.

From this place, sovereignty is no longer a reaction to harm. It is a natural state. You are not sovereign because you were hurt. You are sovereign because you remembered who you are.

You may choose a partnership from here. Or you may choose solitude. Or seasons of both.

Neither path is superior. Neither is a failure.

Sovereignty does not mean isolation. Aligned partnership does not mean self-loss. Both are expressions of the same truth: You will not abandon yourself again.

If love arrives, it will arrive to meet you—not to rescue you. If it does not, your life will still be full, meaningful, creative, and alive.

This is the paradox most people never grasp:

When you stop needing love to complete you, you become capable of receiving real love. Not fantasy. Not potential. Not intensity masquerading as intimacy. But steady love. Kind love. Love that can hold your truth without flinching.

And if such love never comes in human form, something else does.

Peace.

Freedom.

Integrity.

An unshakeable relationship with yourself—and with the unseen intelligence that has guided you through every fire.

You were never meant to be consumed by love.

You were meant to be met by it.

And being met requires you to stand where you are—clearly, visibly, unapologetically. So let this be the final instruction, the one that matters above all others:

Trust what your body tells you. Not what you hope. Not what you're afraid of losing. Not what you've been taught to tolerate.

Trust the sensation.

Trust the contraction.

Trust the ease.

Trust the subtle knowing that arrives before language.

Your body is ancient.

It has survived everything you have lived through.

It knows the difference between danger and growth, between longing and alignment, between love and survival.

And your heart—contrary to what you were told—is not foolish.

The heart is not reckless. It is precise. It does not want drama. It wants truth.

It does not want to be proven worthy. It wants to be honoured. When you honour your heart, you do not harden. You become clear. You become lighter. You become less available to confusion. Less tolerant of distortion. Less willing to trade your life force for crumbs. And in that clarity, something sacred happens.

What is not meant for you falls away—sometimes quietly, sometimes abruptly, but always decisively.

What is meant for you recognises you. This is not mysticism. This is alignment.

So, whether your path leads you into deep partnership or radiant sovereignty, let it be guided by this simple, radical devotion:

To never betray your inner knowing. To never silence your truth to preserve attachment. To never confuse endurance with love again.

You are not here to be tested endlessly. You are not here to be diminished. You are not here to prove your worth through suffering. You are here to live awake. To love consciously. To stand in the quiet authority of someone who knows themselves. And when you do, life meets you differently. People meet you differently. Love meets you differently.

Because the moment you choose yourself without apology, the universe no longer has to break you to wake you. You have already arrived. This is not the end of your story. It is the end of confusion.

And from here on, you walk guided—not by fear, fantasy, or hope—but by the deepest intelligence you possess:

Your intuition. Your heart. Your truth. That is the throne. That is the law.

That is the way home.